ARIZONA'S SCENIC ROADS AND HIKES

Arizona's Scenic Roads & Hikes

Unforgettable Journeys in the Grand Canyon State

ROGER NAYLOR

University of New Mexico Press • Albuquerque

Published 2020
Printed in the United States of America

ISBN 978-0-8263-5927-8 (paper)
ISBN 978-0-8263-5926-1 (electronic)

Library of Congress Control Number:
2020942359

Cover photo: Courtesy of Mike Koopsen, Sedona.
Frontispiece: Courtesy of Mike Koopsen, Sedona.

Map by Mindy Basinger Hill

Composed in Minion Pro and Gotham

TO MY WIFE, MICHELE,

who has made such a wonderful journey possible

with her love, support, insight, and endless patience.

Contents

CENTRAL HIGHLANDS

CENTRAL DESERTS

SOUTHERN ARIZONA

Arizona road trips can be the adventure of a lifetime. Photo by the author.

Arizona Scenic Roads and Highways

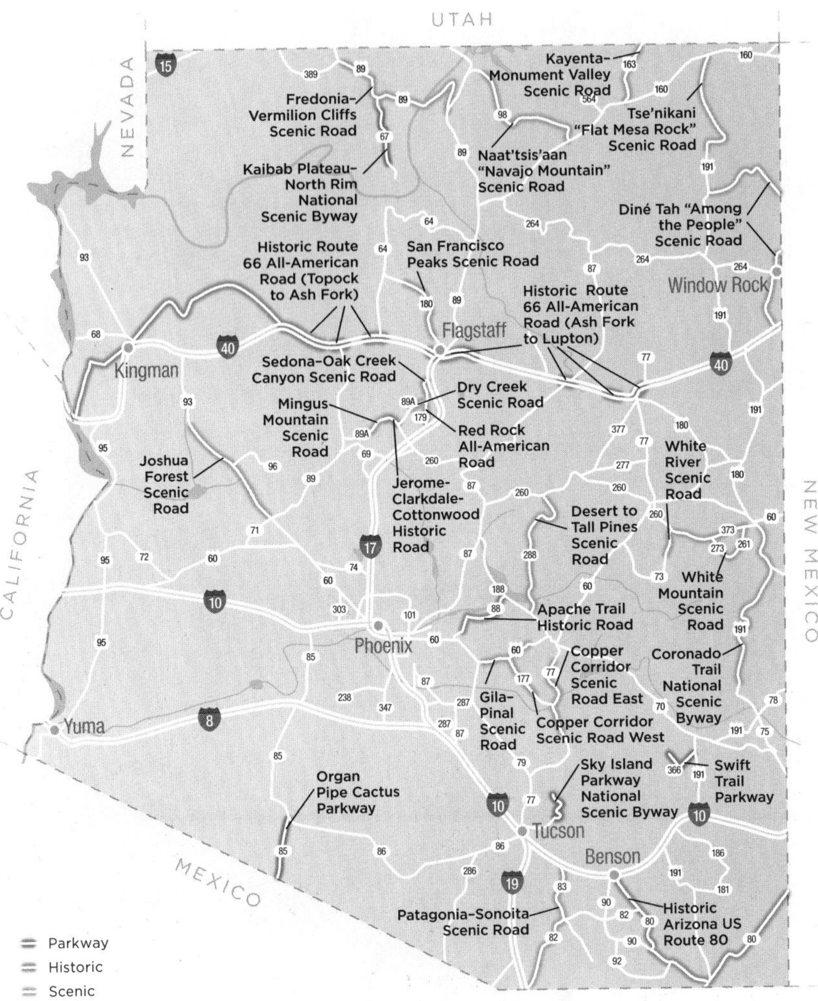

Introduction

Arizona is the only state where you can hike into one of the Seven Natural Wonders of the World.

Not far from the Grand Canyon, you can stand amid alpine tundra—tundra, for crying out loud! It carpets the summit of Humphreys Peak, the state's tallest mountain soaring to an elevation of 12,633 feet. And don't think for a minute that Humphreys is lonely way up there. Arizona has twenty-six peaks that rise above 10,000 feet. It's a surprisingly vertical landscape.

Desert? Absolutely. There's plenty of that, too. Arizona is the only state that contains the Sonoran Desert, a verdant and biologically diverse desert with thriving animal and plant communities, defined by cactus as tall as office buildings. Dropping around to visit the Sonoran and maybe borrow a cup of saguaro cactus fruit are the other three major American deserts—Mojave, Great Basin, and Chihuahuan —making Arizona the only state where you can find elements of all four.

The world's largest contiguous ponderosa pine forest stretches across Arizona. And despite Arizona being an arid state, the nation's largest and second largest man-made lakes—Lake Mead and Lake Powell—stretch along the northern border. No state has more land set aside for Native Americans. When NASA was preparing to land on the moon, Arizona is where they trained.

This is where you'll find the southernmost ski resort and the southernmost mile-high city in America, two of the nation's largest volcanic fields, the longest unbroken stretch of Route 66 still in existence, the best preserved meteor crater on earth, the site of the Old West's bloodiest range war and its most notorious gunfight, the most famous slot canyon in the Southwest, and the world's first International Dark Sky City. This is where you'll find the red rocks of Sedona, the monoliths of Monument Valley, the fossilized trees of Petrified Forest, the otherworldly badlands of the Painted Desert, the legendary fortress of the Superstition Mountains, and the 200-mile long spine of the Mogollon Rim separating the "sky islands" of the southern deserts from the eroded heights of the Colorado Plateau in the north.

To put it mildly, when you go outside to play in Arizona, you're in the big leagues.

Hard to imagine a place more perfectly designed for road trips than Arizona. It's a big old state, the sixth largest in the union, covering nearly 114,000 square

In Arizona, you can hike among cactus as tall as office buildings. Courtesy of Mike Koopsen, Sedona.

A new day begins in Monument Valley. Courtesy of Rick Mortensen, Cincinnati.

miles. Since most of Arizona's population centers are found in clustered bunches, that leaves vast tracts of backcountry for exploring. It's sprinkled with just the right number of small towns to add character and to keep travelers gassed up and well fed. Plus, such varied habitats mean road tripping is a year-round activity in these parts. There are only a handful of days out of the whole year you can't find 70 degrees somewhere in Arizona.

Welcome to my world.

For more than four decades I've rambled around this astonishing state, poking into every nook and cranny. At first it was just for fun because I was swoony in love with everything I saw. Somewhere along the way I turned it into my job. I went from being a freelance writer covering a wide range of topics to an Arizona travel writer, where my beat consisted entirely of the forty-eighth state. And in case you're wondering if it's really cool to get paid to live out your dreams, the answer is yes. Yes, it is.

So let me show you around my home. Dip your wheels into amazing Arizona. We'll start by driving every state-designated highway. There are twenty-seven of them, divided into different categories—nineteen Scenic Roads, four Historic Roads, and four Parkways. Of these, five of the roads also have a federal designation as National Scenic Byways or All-American Roads.

Road Designations

The Arizona Department of Transportation oversees the designating and planning of scenic roads. Here are the guidelines they use.

Scenic Roads

These include a roadway (or segment of a roadway) that has a memorable visual impression, is free of visual encroachment, and forms a harmonious composite of visual patterns.

Arizona has nineteen Scenic Roads. My five personal favorites are:

Sedona–Oak Creek Canyon Scenic Road
Kayenta–Monument Valley Scenic Road
Fredonia–Vermilion Cliffs Scenic Road
Patagonia–Sonoita Scenic Road
White Mountain Scenic Road

Historic Roads

These include a roadway (or segment of a roadway) that has historical importance to the state, nation, or region; is easily accessible; and has uniqueness.

The Historic Roads in Arizona are:

Historic Route 66 (also an All-American Road)
Apache Trail Historic Road
Jerome-Clarkdale-Cottonwood Historic Road
Historic Arizona US Route 80

Parkways

These include a roadway (or segment of a roadway) that meets scenic or historic road criteria, has a 1-mile minimum distance between access roads, allows visitor facilities/interpretive areas, and offers controlled access to adjacent development.

The Parkways in Arizona are:

Sky Island Parkway (also a National Scenic Byway)
Kaibab Plateau–North Rim Parkway (also a National Scenic Byway)
Swift Trail Parkway
Organ Pipe Cactus Parkway

National Scenic Byways

These include a roadway (or segment of a roadway) that must be a currently designated state scenic road, has multistate significance, contains no gaps in continuity, accommodates bicycles and pedestrians, has a completed Corridor Management Plan, and possesses one or more of the following intrinsic qualities: scenic, historic, recreational, cultural, archeological, or natural.

Arizona has three National Scenic Byways:

Kaibab Plateau–North Rim National Scenic Byway

Sky Island Parkway National Scenic Byway

Coronado Trail National Scenic Byway

All-American Roads

These include a roadway that meets the criteria of a National Scenic Byway, but with the following additional requirements: has national significance instead of multistate significance, possesses multiple intrinsic qualities, and be considered a destination unto itself.

Arizona has two All-American Roads:

Red Rock All-American Road

Historic Route 66 All-American Road (Topock to Ash Fork and Ash Fork to Lupton)

The Arizona landscape is filled with surprising sights like the sparkling canyon-cradled waters of Lake Powell. Courtesy of Mike Koopsen, Sedona.

Every paved highway into Sedona is an officially designated scenic road. Courtesy of Mike Koopsen, Sedona.

These are the very best Arizona has to offer. We'll travel to ancient Native American villages, old Mormon settlements, cow towns, mining camps, swimming holes, ghost towns, wildlife parks, state parks, forts, museums, art galleries, roadside attractions, trading posts, wineries overlooking a creek, wineries on grassy hills, and swinging-door saloons. Along the way we'll visit a town run by burros, drink from a river that will prompt a lifetime of lies, listen for the howl of wolves in the forest, marvel at sunsets, sleep in a teepee-shaped motel room, and stand on a corner in Winslow, Arizona, just like in the song. We'll climb towering mountains, cross sagebrush plains and grassy prairies, delve into craggy canyons, traverse sun-scorched deserts, follow tumbling streams, and skirt a surprising number of lakes. What's up with all the lakes?

These are the road trips of America's youth, before the incursion of the interstate system changed forever how we traveled. Set out on a ribbon of pavement and aim for the horizon in search of delight and wonder. So let's jump in the car, roll the windows down, crank up the radio, and just go, baby, go!

Each road features attractions and activities, and I have tried to describe as many as I could, as well as some locally owned places to eat and sleep. So whether you're making a quick jaunt or spending the weekend, I've got you covered. Along with the twenty-seven official roads, I include several adjacent highways that are often just as spectacular. These make great side trips delivering more scenery, history, and other points of interest.

With each road, I've included the official parameters such as starting and ending milepost markers. Of course, that doesn't mean much in the real world. Many of these segments begin or end in isolated locales. But until we perfect some sort of teleportation app on our phones, travelers will still set out from the nearest city or town and that's how I write the description. In many cases the scenic roads can be combined with others to form a loop or longer journeys can be pieced together, and I have attempted to point out the various possibilities. Remember that mileages specified are approximate—odometer readings can vary from vehicle to vehicle.

If you do nothing but make these stunning drives, you'll rack up countless adventures and plenty of great memories. But I want you to fall in love with Arizona like I did—first by driving all over the place and consuming the scenery in big voracious gulps, and then by stopping and studying the details. I'm a hiker at heart. On any road trip, I like to walk around. Maybe you do too.

So I've paired each road with a handful of nearby hiking trails. Most range from easy to moderate, although there are some challenging ones. It's just a chance for you to climb out of the vehicle and stretch your legs. Slow the pace down and see things up close and personal.

With each hiking trail I tried to provide all necessary details including contact information if a managing agency is involved. Yet obviously these are mere thumbnail sketches designed to spark your interest. It's always a good idea before going on a hike to get up-to-date information including weather and trail conditions.

The numbered trails are on national forest land. Most, although not all, forest trails are given a number. Trails that are city-owned or located in national parks, state parks, etc. don't have a number.

Hiking Trail Safety and Etiquette

Always tell someone your plans. Let someone know where you'll be hiking and when you expect to return.

Do your homework. Know the weather forecast and don't hesitate to turn back if conditions take a turn for the worse.

Don't overdo it. Know your physical abilities and limitations, and don't push beyond them. Hiking is great exercise anyway, so keep it at a level that's enjoyable.

Dress appropriately. Wear comfortable but sturdy footwear, a wide-brimmed hat, and sunglasses. Be sure to slather on the sunscreen.

A winter hush falls over West Fork Trail deep within Oak Creek Canyon. Courtesy of Mike Koopsen, Sedona.

Carry plenty of water. The only way to battle Arizona's arid climate is by staying hydrated. Take water with you even on short hikes and plan to carry up to a gallon per person on longer outings.

Take the essentials. Make sure your daypack is stocked with a few basic items like a first-aid kit, flashlight, compass, map, snacks, whistle, signal mirror, and knife.

Stay on the trail. Short cuts and stray paths speed erosion and trample fragile vegetation.

Don't disturb anything. Leave rocks, plants, and artifacts just as you find them.

Pack out all your trash. All of it, no matter how small.

Respect wildlife. Never feed or disturb any animals you might encounter.

Be prepared before starting out on any road trip. Many of these highways are well traveled, but some head into remote isolated country. Cell-phone service can be unreliable. Not every small settlement has a gas station or ATM. Gas up before starting out and never let the tank get too low. Make sure you have cash

Welcome to the Grand Canyon State. Prepare to be amazed. Photo by the author.

on hand for minor emergencies and because not every roadside vendor takes plastic. You don't want to miss out on possibly the greatest street tacos of your life because you didn't have a fiver.

Always carry food items and extra water. Just for emphasis, always carry water. Make sure your spare tire is inflated. Carry a map or gazetteer. Do not rely solely on GPS. This is a land veined with impassable old mining roads and jeep tracks that can appear on GPS systems as inviting little shortcuts. Watch for wildlife and critters that are not so wild. Much of Arizona is open range, so cows are technically big slow pedestrians.

The most important thing to take along on any road trip comes standard issue with every vehicle and is located on the floorboard right next to the gas pedal. Don't be afraid to apply the brake liberally. You're not on the interstate; stop wherever you want. Stop for a viewpoint or an overlook. Stop to watch a rowdy gathering of clouds waft over a mesa. Stop for a food truck or to read a roadside marker. Stop to take a photo of a faded sign. Stop because the late afternoon sun bathes the bristly spines of a teddy bear cholla in a golden light that seems to glow from within and for an instant it feels like the most magical thing you've ever seen. Every time you stop or stutter step or circle back, you're putting your own unique stamp on this road trip; you're seeing it in a way it's never been seen before.

How I envy you. Happy motoring!

NORTH CENTRAL

A winding mountain road passes through the forests atop Mingus Mountain separating Prescott and the Verde Valley. Photo by the author.

Mingus Mountain Scenic Road

Overview Connecting Prescott and Jerome, the road rises from windswept grasslands and climbs across the broad back of Mingus Mountain where expansive vistas take in the Verde Valley and the high ledge of the Colorado Plateau.

Route Numbers Arizona State Highway 89A.

Mileage The scenic road is 11.5 miles (Milepost 332 to Milepost 343.5). It is 35 miles from Prescott to Jerome.

Special Notes Expect mountain grades, sharp curves, and steep drop-offs. Winter weather conditions are possible at the higher elevations. This road connects to Jerome-Clarkdale-Cottonwood Historic Road.

Travel Note The Sharlot Hall Museum preserves the Territorial Governor's Mansion, an elegant log cabin that still stands in its original position. The museum is named for Sharlot Mabridth Hall, a writer and poet who became the first woman to hold office in Arizona when she was appointed Territorial Historian in 1909.

In 1900, a raging fire swept through Prescott's famed Whiskey Row. As flames threatened the Palace Saloon, heroic patrons sprang into action. Almost without thinking, they hoisted up the large ornate Brunswick bar and carried it through the swinging doors out into the street. Then they resumed tossing back the hooch.

Now that's a drinking story! And for the record, even though it's just a nickname, Whiskey Row is one of the all-time great street names.

Prescott began as a gold camp and was declared the territorial capital of Arizona in 1864. It's a thoroughly Western town but with a comfortable Eastern feel. A stately courthouse surrounded by a tree-shaded plaza anchors one of the loveliest downtowns in Arizona. Elegant Victorian homes line the streets fronted by tidy yards overflowing with flowers. You don't earn the title "Everybody's Hometown" without bringing a heavy measure of charm to the table. The downtown is a treasure trove of art galleries, antique shops, restaurants, quaint B&Bs, and, of course, enough saloons to keep the spirit (and spirits) of Whiskey Row alive—including the Palace, rebuilt the year after the big fire. Opened in 1877, the Palace Restaurant and Saloon is Arizona's oldest bar.

A big part of what makes Prescott special is the recreational opportunities. Long regarded as a popular retirement community, Prescott has also been rediscovered by a new generation of mountain bikers, rock climbers, kayakers, trail runners, and hikers.

The town nestles in a forested bowl, 5,374 feet above sea level at the edge of the Bradshaw Mountains, and wears a chain of lakes like a sapphire necklace. As you head north from downtown on 89, you'll pass picturesque Watson Lake, sparkling blue amid piles of tawny boulders known as the Granite Dells. There are some free parking spots overlooking the lake and a park that offers picnic areas, restrooms, boat launches, seasonal camping, and a series of linked hiking trails circling the water.

While Arizona 89 heads almost due north from Prescott toward Chino Valley, turn onto 89A, which branches off to the east. It crosses the grasslands of Prescott Valley where pronghorn graze amid lonely suburbs. The high wall of the Black Hills looms overhead, and as you reach the woodlands at the mouth of Yeager Canyon, the Mingus Mountain Scenic Road begins.

Trying to choose the most scenic road in Arizona is an impossible task. The state bristles with highway panoramas. A drive to the market can reveal numerous heart-squeezing sights. Yet if someone were to declare Arizona 89A as the state's most scenic road overall, such a claim would generate few arguments. The 90-mile highway runs from Prescott to Flagstaff. In that short stretch it contains four specially designated drives—Mingus Mountain Scenic Road, Jerome-Clarkdale-Cottonwood Historic Road, Dry Creek Scenic Road, and Sedona–Oak Creek Canyon Scenic Road. That's a lot of eye-popping bang for your buck.

It's nice to know you're on the cusp of something special as you start threading your way up Yeager Canyon. Oaks and junipers crowd the road early on, but tall ponderosa pines soon dominate. The tight curves and switchbacks make this a popular run for anyone in a sports car or astride a Harley. Carsick-prone kids might perceive it differently. There are several pullouts to offer respite for queasy stomachs or nervous passengers. As someone who spent a good part of my childhood decorating the shoulders of curvy roads with the remains of breakfast, I always find pullouts a welcome sight.

The road continues upward through heavy forest until it reaches a high pass separating Mingus Mountain and Woodchute Mountain. At approximately 7,800 feet, Mingus Mountain is the highest point in the Black Hills. Where the road crests, you've got a couple of options. To the left is Forest Road 106 (unsigned) that leads to Potato Patch Campground and Woodchute Trail (see Hiking). A right turn puts you on FR 104. The dirt road is suitable for sedans as it ambles back to Mingus Campground, picnic areas, and Mingus Lake, which is merely a pond with dreams but is stocked with rainbow trout. There are a couple of viewpoints, some hiking trails, and a popular launch site for hang gliders.

While Mingus is not the tallest or most distinctive Arizona mountain, it has something more important than any of that. It is my own personal backyard mountain. For me (and everyone else who lives in this part of the Verde Valley), Mingus defines the western horizon.

This is not a unique situation. Arizona is a surprisingly vertical landscape. The state contains 3,928 mountain peaks and summits—more than any other Mountain State—so plenty of residents have their own landmass dominating the skyline. There are few places in Arizona that don't include mountain views.

It's easy to form a connection with our mountains as we watch them reflect the seasons and change moods throughout the day. During winter I can track the snow level by how low the veil of white descends on the flank of Mingus. In summer, those high ramparts tempt me with the promise of cooler temperatures and the perfume of pines. During the monsoon, I watch the mountain swaddle itself in dark scowling clouds.

More than anything else, Mingus Mountain initiates my sunsets. Thousands of times I have watched from my porch as a weary sun collapses atop the summit, resting for the length of a long sigh and then slipping beyond the soft embrace. Sometimes they are quiet, discreet affairs, a quick flash of golden light and it's over. But more often than not, they are big brassy sunsets, drenched in color. Arizona sunsets can be so shocking they make birds fly into lampposts and butterflies turn to strong drink. They give well-bred ladies the vapors and cause hoboes to jump from moving trains. It's a show that never grows stale.

While you're on the summit of Mingus Mountain, don't forget to wave at my house some 4,000 feet below. Even if you can't see

Jerome, a mining town turned arts community, clings to steep slopes in the Black Hills. Courtesy of Mike Koopsen, Sedona.

me standing on my porch waving back, it's still an enticing view. A lot of geological drama is squeezed into the panorama that includes the Mogollon Rim, the San Francisco Peaks, the red cliffs of Sedona, and the meandering line of the Verde River.

The descent proves just as steep and curving as the climb up the mountain. But since you're no longer hemmed in by a canyon, the panoramas are more expansive. Take advantage of the pullouts to stop and marvel at the details. You'll see evidence of mining activity as you get lower. Pass through a rocky cleft, then wind around a few more curves and you'll be pulling into Jerome. Once a booming mining camp, Jerome is now a thriving artist haven. It clings to the mountain slope a mile in the air. This marks the end of Mingus Mountain Scenic Road and the beginning of the Jerome-Clarkdale-Cottonwood Historic Road.

Hiking

GRANITE GARDENS

This rumpled series of loops makes a great introduction to Prescott's most distinctive feature, the Granite Dells, a massive field of exposed bedrock gnawed by erosion. It's a great kid-friendly hike, but why should they have all the fun? You'll clamber across boulders following painted white dots. Soon you're climbing an actual thirty-eight-step staircase in the middle of nowhere, an impressive engineering feat from the Over the Hill Gang. The all-volunteer group works tirelessly building and maintaining Prescott trails. Circle the dome-like formation of Castle Rock and then catch your breath on a bench bearing the words "Go outside and play." After crossing a narrow grassy cleft, the trail scrambles back into the granite, weaving among weirdly shaped rock piles and even squeezing through a narrow grotto. It drops back down to the little valley, which will be your exit point after 1.5 miles. Now aren't you glad you came outside to play? Trailhead is off Granite Gardens Drive, a dirt road off Arizona 89 between Mileposts 317–18 (across from Granite Gate Senior Living Community). (928) 777-1590, www.prescotttrails.com.

Historic buildings and picturesque ruins line the hilly streets of Jerome. Courtesy of Mike Koopsen, Sedona.

WOODCHUTE TRAIL #102

This trail is all about big vistas as it follows an old bulldozer track into the Woodchute Wilderness. When Jerome mines were humming, big ponderosa pines were harvested from these slopes for shoring timbers and transported by chute to the loading platform for the narrow-gauge railroad. The trail rambles through mixed forest and crosses a narrow saddle with views stretching in all directions. It enters the wilderness and climbs to the summit of Woodchute Mountain; the last half-mile is a fairly steep slog. While the trail continues down the other side to the former railroad, now Forest Road 318, most day hikers use this high perch as a turnaround point for a round-trip hike of just under 7 miles. At Mingus Pass, turn north onto FR 106, make a quick turn onto FR 106D and continue 0.7 miles to the trailhead. (928) 567-4121, www.fs.usda.gov/prescott.

GADDES CANYON TRAIL #110

Starting near the old lookout tower close to the summit campground off FR 104, Gaddes Canyon Trail doesn't offer the views of the surrounding countryside as do the more exposed trails scrambling down the sides of Mingus. It stays mostly in the shade, making for a comfortable hike during the summer. The trail drops gently into Gaddes Canyon. A small spring adds a bit of lushness to the canyon bottom. Oak, walnut, and pine trees create a pleasant canopy of green. The trail climbs from the canyon to a low ridge across open terrain. Keep an eye peeled for deer in this parklike setting. The last section drops down to join Allen Springs Road, for a 5.2-mile round-trip hike. (928) 567-4121, www.fs.usda.gov/prescott.

Where to Eat and Stay

THE LOCAL, PRESCOTT

Start your day healthy and happy at this eatery where nearly every item is prepared using non-processed, organic, and locally sourced ingredients. Breakfast is served all day, featuring traditional favorites with a twist. The Southwest Sunrise is a spin on eggs Benedict, featuring a stack of complementary flavors and textures highlighted by the house-made ginger aioli. 520 W. Sheldon St., (928) 237-4724, www.localprescott.com.

GRAPES RESTAURANT & BAR, JEROME

A charming Italian eatery, Grapes specializes in pizzas, lunchtime sandwiches, and heaping pasta bowls you create yourself. Most entrees come with a suggested wine pairing. The sourdough zinburger is a house favorite—Angus beef drizzled with red zinfandel and topped with bacon, provolone, and herbed mayo. Enjoy a Jerome street scene when you dine at a table on the patio. They also offer nightly specials on weekdays. 111 Main St., (928) 639-8477, www.grapesjerome.com.

MOTOR LODGE, PRESCOTT

This historic property strikes a balance of eye-pleasing nostalgia and modern comfort. A dozen units are clustered in the shape of a skinny horseshoe and painted with a snappy color scheme. Rooms are spotlessly clean and effortlessly cool, sporting an eclectic mix of furnishings and art that samples a range of eras. Quality of the bedding, towels, and other amenities will conjure up far pricier resorts. A small porch fronts each room where guests tend to gather in the afternoons with conversations bouncing back and forth. It's nice to be reminded that this is how people used to travel. 503 S. Montezuma St., (928) 717-0157, www.themotorlodge.com.

CONNOR HOTEL, JEROME

When Jerome reinvented itself from mining ghost town to artist haven, the Connor Hotel did likewise. Built in 1898, the décor today combines comfortable Victorian with modern amenities and artistic flourishes. The Connor offers a dozen beautifully restored rooms and even a few moaning ghosts. The Spirit Room occupies the ground level of the Connor Hotel, where bands kick out the jams many evenings and on Saturday and Sunday afternoons. Only one hundred people can squeeze into the Spirit Room and seating is scarce, but when things get righteously thumping who wants a chair anyway? 160 Main St., (928) 634-5006, www.connorhotel.com.

When You Go

Prescott Chamber of Commerce Visitor Center: 117 W. Goodwin St., (928) 445-2000, www.prescott.org.

Palace Restaurant & Saloon: 120 S. Montezuma St., (928) 541-1996, www.historicpalace.com.

Sharlot Hall Museum: Fee. 415 W. Gurley St., (928) 445-3122, www.sharlothallmuseum.org.

Potato Patch Campground: Fee. (928) 567-4121, www.fs.usda.gov/prescott.

Mingus Campground: Fee. (928) 567-4121, www.fs.usda.gov/prescott.

Jerome Chamber of Commerce: (928) 634-2900, www.jeromechamber.com.

Historic 89A offers splendid views of the Verde Valley as it curves down the slopes to Clarkdale and Cottonwood. Courtesy of Mike Koopsen, Sedona.

Jerome-Clarkdale-Cottonwood Historic Road

Overview This road stitches together the mining history of the region and explores how each of the intertwined communities has evolved. Today, it's a traveler's dream highlighting art galleries, museums, wine-tasting rooms, an excursion railroad, ancient Indian dwellings, and the tree-lined Verde River.

Route Numbers Arizona State Highway 89A.

Mileage The historic road is 10 miles (Milepost 343.5 to Milepost 348, and Milepost 348 to Milepost 353.5).

Special Notes This is one of four Historic Roads in the state. A series of twisting curves leading up the mountainside makes this a popular ride for motorcyclists. It connects with Mingus Mountain Scenic Road and Dry Creek Scenic Road.

The April sun glints off the chrome of the motorcycles lined up in front of the Spirit Room. The door is flung open wide and music spills into the street, full-on rock and roll with a hint of a country twang that gets everybody dancing. It's a small bar but since live bands still perform most evenings and on weekend afternoons, it's always jumping. The wooden dance floor by the stage is scuffed dark and shiny as if it were carved from black onyx.

At nearby Paul and Jerry's Saloon, folks stand two and three deep at the bar. A duo plays in the back corner with the singer belting out one bluesy ballad about heartache and loss after another, with just enough of a tremble in her powerful voice to make us all hate the man who so obviously wronged her. I'm two tequila shots away from punching the guitarist, just in case he turns out to be the jerk.

Sidewalks are crowded with tourists. Arm-wrapped couples, families, and roving gangs of seniors stream in and out of the art galleries, wine-tasting rooms, and restaurants all housed in historic buildings. For a ghost town, Jerome sure feels vibrant this fine spring afternoon. And we owe it all to hippies.

Jerome teeters a mile in the air clinging

to the steep slope of Cleopatra Hill and overlooking the Verde Valley with views stretching to the sandstone cliffs of Sedona and the San Francisco Peaks some 60 miles distant. It was once known as the "Billion-Dollar Mining Camp" for the incredible wealth pulled from the ground. Prospectors filed the first claims in 1876, later selling out to the United Verde Copper Company backed by New York financier Eugene Jerome. Even though he never visited, his money did and that was enough to name the ramshackle camp in his honor.

The rugged terrain made everything more complicated, from hauling in equipment to transporting ore. In 1888, Jerome sold the operation to William A. Clark, a US Senator from Montana and a copper mogul with deep pockets. Clark used his fortune to build a narrow-gauge railway, and the United Verde became the largest-producing copper mine in Arizona Territory.

The boom continued with two flourishing mines, the United Verde and the Little Daisy owned by James S. Douglas, well into the 1920s. At one time, 15,000 residents were squeezed into the bawdy camp known for a high concentration of saloons and brothels. Production slowed and prices dropped during the Great Depression. The Little Daisy shuttered in 1938. After the United Verde closed in 1953, fewer than fifty people remained.

Jerome hung on as a rickety ghost town for several years before it was finally discovered by enterprising hippies. They moved in, opened businesses, and spruced up the place while preserving the historic integrity of the structures scattered across the hills. More artists arrived and a communal spirit took hold. With the bounty of art, a spectacular setting, panoramic views, and good music and food, Jerome has turned into one of Arizona's best day trips. Hippies . . . is there anything they can't do?

Travel Note James Douglas, known as "Rawhide Jimmy," built a rambling 8,700-square-foot mansion on the hill above his mine. Today, it is Jerome State Historic Park, a stylish museum filled with artifacts and exhibits of the town's wild heyday.

Arizona 89A winds through the narrow streets of Jerome, leaving town via a hog-back ridge with houses hanging off the edge. You sweep around the old high school, now a collection of art galleries, and drop sharply toward the valley floor. Views are spectacular, gazing across the valley to the canyons and cliffs of Sedona and the mountains of Flagstaff. Languid curves snake through soft hills dotted with cacti and fat stalks of agaves.

At the traffic circle at the bottom of the hill, stay on Historic 89A and continue straight ahead toward Clarkdale. Turning right will lead you to Cottonwood via the bypass. Surely "bypass" is the cruelest word in the lexicon of small towns. Their only purpose seems to be to steer you away from the good stuff.

Clarkdale was Arizona's first company town. While mines were still booming in Jerome, a vein of high-grade ore was discovered beneath the smelter, so a new one had to be built. Construction began on the valley floor, not just of a smelter but also of an entirely new town. Clarkdale—named after William Clark—was designed with precision planning and technological advancements such as electricity, sewer, and copper water piping that were far from the norm in the early 1900s.

Sturdy brick homes fronted by tidy yards surround a quaint downtown. The centerpiece property is a grassy park anchored by a large gazebo. This swath of green space, used daily by residents and the site of all events and celebrations, serves as the heart

Summer clouds are reflected in the lagoons of Dead Horse Ranch State Park. Photo by the author.

and soul of Clarkdale. It instills the community with a small-town-America, hipster-Mayberry vibe so cherished by residents and visitors alike.

The one-block downtown includes a handful of businesses and a couple of intriguing museums. The Clarkdale Historical Society & Museum provides a comprehensive picture of the town's past. In the Copper Art Museum you'll find over 5,000 objects made from copper and its alloys, everything from architecture to drinkware to religious artifacts.

Clarkdale is also home to the Verde Canyon Railroad, an excursion train making a 40-mile round trip into a remote wilderness, nestled between two national forests at the confluence of desert and wetland. Traveling the same track once used to haul Jerome ore from the smelter, the train rolls through a lush riparian corridor carved by the Verde River. Coach and first-class accommodations are available, and all cars provide access to open-air viewing platforms that are impossible to resist.

Outside of Clarkdale, Tuzigoot National Monument, an ancient Sinagua pueblo, crowns a limestone hill overlooking the Verde River. The terraced village consisted of 110 rooms, including second- and third-story structures. The National Park Service restored one dwelling so visitors can experience what life was like for the Sinagua who resided here between AD 1000 and 1400.

Travel Note The Sinagua people were mining the rugged hills centuries before the first Anglo prospectors. They used some of the minerals to trade and for making jewelry and other items.

Soon you're entering Old Town Cottonwood. Originally the area was a farming community supplying goods to the soldiers of Camp Verde and later the miners of Jerome. Cottonwood developed a mercantile trade as the copper mines of Jerome kept producing. Folks wanting to start a business, own some property, or those who simply chafed under the regulations imposed by a company town migrated to Cottonwood.

Today, I'm happy to report that Cottonwood feels vibrant again. For a lot of years, Old Town was seriously underutilized. Despite a postcard quaint setting, many of the Prohibition-era buildings fronted by covered sidewalks sat vacant or were full of thrift-shop goods. That began to change when one couple, Eric and Michelle Jurisin, opened an upscale restaurant in the middle of Old Town and later a more casual but still stylish eatery across the street. And they hung on.

Other businesses eventually moved in. Things really took off when several wine-tasting rooms opened (see Dry Creek Scenic Road to discover vineyards right outside of town) and Cottonwood became a destination for oenophiles. Suddenly, my little burg was hip. Now Old Town supports a great collection of galleries, shops, restaurants, hotels, and wineries just a stone's throw from the Verde River. Despite the livelier atmosphere, that small-town charm remains. I still occasionally see horses tied up on Main Street, while cowpokes dine at a sidewalk café.

You'll continue through the rest of Cottonwood, which still serves as a retail center for the surrounding communities. Just before the end of the historic road, you'll pass the turn off to Dead Horse Ranch State Park with fishing lagoons, a long section of the Verde River, horseback rides, and a network of some of the best hiking and biking trails in the valley.

Hiking

JAIL TRAIL

Starting right in the heart of Old Town Cottonwood, this mile-long trail burrows into a leafy riparian tangle and makes a quick visit to the Verde River. The path leads past the old jail constructed of river rock, and travels through the shade of willows and cottonwood trees as it quickly reaches the water lined by cattails. Continue downstream across a rocky flood plain. You have the option of continuing to Dead Horse Ranch State Park or just enjoying the music of flowing water and birdsong and returning the way you came. Look for the "Gateway to the Verde River" arch and park in the lot on the right at 1101 N. Main St.

DEAD HORSE RANCH STATE PARK

Over 20 miles of trails crisscross this park nestled on the banks of the river and extend into the limestone hills. There are plenty of short easy hikes to choose from, such as Tavasci Marsh Trail (1 mile) and the sandy Verde River Greenway Trail (2 miles). Longer routes leave the park boundary and venture into the national forest land. You can put some nice loops together suitable for hikers and mountain bikers, such as Lime Kiln–Thumper–Lower Raptor or Lower Raptor–Bones, both about 7 miles. Fee. (928) 634-5283, www.azstateparks.com.

CLIFFROSE TRAIL

Sitting on the edge of Cottonwood, the Cliffrose Trail is part of a regional effort to add more paths to make open space more accessible and bind communities together. A trailhead provides parking off the Mingus Avenue Extension, a quarter-mile from 89A, just east of Cottonwood. The trail loops around the limestone hills, skirting the edge of a ravine with good views in all directions. It also connects to an old jeep road that heads east, stretching across national forest land. Don't expect much in the way of signage once you're on the Cliffrose—and the multiple pathways can be confusing. But it's hard to get lost with the red cliffs of Sedona in the northeast, the rising bulk of Mingus Mountain to the west, and both 89A and Mingus Extension often visible.

Where to Eat and Stay

NIC'S ITALIAN STEAK & CRAB HOUSE, COTTONWOOD

This is the restaurant that paved the way for the resurgence of Old Town. An upscale eatery that served prime filets, seafood, and fine wine and was only open for dinner forced people to see Old Town in a different light. Nic's is reminiscent of an East Coast restaurant with lots of dark wood, polished brass, and an authentic New England clam chowder. The Jurisins created a gathering spot with quality food and atmosphere, and the community sprang up around them. 925 N. Main St., (928) 634-9626, www.nicsaz.com.

GHOST CITY INN, JEROME

Built around 1890 as a boardinghouse for mine managers, the two-story building now operates as a delightful bed-and-breakfast. Walk out your door, and you're in the heart of Jerome. Each of the six well-appointed rooms maintains a different theme, all tied to local history or geography. Enjoy expansive landscape views from the verandas during the day and the canopy of stars that settles over the Verde Valley each night. A bountiful breakfast is served in the sunny dining room. 541 N. Main St., (928) 634-4678, www.ghostcityinn.com.

The town of Cottonwood stretches along the base of Mingus Mountain and the Black Hills. Photo by the author.

IRON HORSE INN, COTTONWOOD

This boutique hotel is one of the great success stories of Old Town Cottonwood. The beautiful motor court built in the 1930s had gone through many changes over the decades and had been in a state of decline when it was purchased and given a loving restoration. New rooms contain elegant touches like plush linens and flat-screen televisions, while maintaining their historic charm. Hang out in the courtyard with the fountains and flowers until you're ready to explore the rest of Old Town. No elevators, so request a downstairs room if needed. 1034 N. Main St., (928) 634-8031, www.ironhorseoldtown.com.

When You Go

Jerome Chamber of Commerce: (928) 634-2900, www.jeromechamber.com.

Spirit Room: 166 Main St., (928) 634-8809, www.spiritroom.com.

Paul and Jerry's Saloon: 206 Main St., (928) 634-2603.

Jerome State Historic Park: Fee. (928) 634-5381, www.azstateparks.com.

Experience Clarkdale: www.experienceclarkdale.com.

Clarkdale Historical Society & Museum: Fee. 900 First North St., (928) 649-1198, www.clarkdalemuseum.org.

Copper Art Museum: Fee. 849 Main St., (928) 649-1858, www.copperartmuseum.com.

Verde Canyon Railroad: Fee. 300 N. Broadway, (800) 582-7245, www.verdecanyonrr.com.

Tuzigoot National Monument: Fee. (928) 634-5564, www.nps.gov/tuzi.

Old Town Cottonwood: (928) 634-7593, www.oldtown.org.

Cottonwood Chamber of Commerce: 849 Cove Parkway, (928) 634-7593, www.cottonwoodchamberaz.org.

Dry Creek Scenic Road

Overview Make a short drive across the fertile Verde Valley from Cottonwood to the red rock landscape of Sedona with plenty of options to extend the journey to other corners of the region.

Route Numbers Arizona State Highway 89A.

Mileage The scenic road is 6.5 miles (Milepost 363.5 to Milepost 370). It is 17 miles from Cottonwood to Sedona.

Special Notes This road provides access to Jerome-Clarkdale-Cottonwood Historic Road and Sedona-Oak Creek Canyon Scenic Road.

The problem with this journey is that it's over much too soon. Fortunately, it connects to several great side trips, so what begins as a quick morning drive can last a weekend if you're so inclined.

As a Cottonwood resident, this is my commute for plenty of mundane errands in Sedona. I drive this road to get a haircut, shop at the pet store, or take in a movie. So it would seem easy to take the half-hour drive for granted. Trust me when I say that's rarely the case. For those few quiet minutes behind the wheel, I get to experience again all the things I love about living in the Verde Valley.

Arizona 89A crosses the Verde River on its way out of Cottonwood. Just before the stoplight at Cornville Road, it turns into a smooth four-lane divided highway and begins a gentle climb through sun-kissed

Travel Note Cottonwood sits at an elevation of 3,320 feet, Sedona is at 4,500 feet and you can join the Mile High Club in Jerome (5,246 feet), assuming you've got a room on an upper floor.

grasslands. Within a couple of miles, as you cross Spring Creek, the open pasture gives way to rolling hills sprinkled with juniper. Above the hilltops, you'll continually spot flirty little glimpses of Sedona's red rocks. In the rearview mirror, Cottonwood is strung along the base of Mingus Mountain while the clustered buildings of Jerome cling to the high shoulder of Cleopatra Hill midway up the slopes.

About 6 miles from Cottonwood, Page Springs Road branches to the south. This is one of those side trips to enjoy later, a tour through wine country. The officially designated scenic road—a mere nubbin at 6.5 miles—begins soon after the Page Springs turn. A paved parking area advertises a scenic view. And it is a nice horizon-filling panorama that stretches from the green-clad slopes of Casner Mountain on the left to the rounded dome of Capitol Butte, also known as Thunder Mountain. Yet this is a mere taste of what's to come.

Formations continue to grow larger in your windshield as you approach Sedona. On the north side of the road lies Sedona Wetlands Preserve, a twenty-seven-acre collection of ponds of treated effluent water ringed by walking paths and cottonwoods. The popular birding spot is open to the public.

The road dips and crosses Dry Creek. Don't bother looking for an actual flowing stream. The name was not bestowed ironically. It only displays moisture during spring runoff or following a powerful monsoon storm.

Past the Sedona Shadows, a small over-fifty-five community, the road begins a final short climb to the city limits. Just beyond Milepost 368, Lower Red Rock Loop Road branches off to the right. Since it's only another couple of miles to the outskirts of West Sedona on 89A, I recommend turning onto Lower Red Rock Loop, which offers some additional sights. The winding 7-mile road circles the base of Schuerman Mountain and curves past the distinctive profile of Cathedral Rock before swinging back around to join 89A.

The always photogenic Cathedral Rock is accessible from Upper Red Rock Loop Road. Courtesy of Mike Koopsen, Sedona.

Coffee Pot Rock looms over West Sedona. Courtesy of Mike Koopsen, Sedona.

Lower Red Rock Loop travels through scrubby hills and begins to drop toward Oak Creek. At 3 miles you reach Red Rock State Park, a 286-acre nature preserve with a network of hiking trails, picnic areas, and a shady patio swarming with hummingbirds. The visitor center includes informative exhibits, and they offer guided hikes and educational programs.

Beyond the park, the road continues skirting the flank of Schuerman Mountain as it winds past a few homesteads. The mountain is named for early settlers in the area. In fact, it was Heinrich and Dorette Schuerman who first got the grape rolling on the local wine scene. They arrived in 1884 and planted an orchard and vineyard along the creek. A few years later they were selling apples, peaches, and wine to loggers in Flagstaff and the miners in Jerome.

Past Loy Lane, the road becomes Upper Red Rock Loop Road. Soon, Cathedral Rock rises above the trees along the banks of the creek. For a closer look—a more familiar look—turn right at the stop sign onto Chavez Ranch Road and follow the signs to Crescent Moon Picnic Site, more commonly known as Red Rock Crossing. Now operated by the forest service concessionaire, this was near the old Schuerman spread. Paths lead down to the stream that meanders past the formation and through forested groves. This is one of the most photographed spots in the Southwest where shutterbugs capture the iconic image of water flowing in front of Cathedral Rock. The shallow creek spills across stony shelves and in a couple of places deepens enough to form inviting little swimming holes. Along with picnic tables, restrooms and drinking water are available at Crescent Moon.

Returning to the loop, the road twists uphill in a series of tight curves. There are a couple of pullouts if you want to enjoy a last look at Cathedral along with Courthouse Butte and other clustered formations.

Passing the high school, the loop ends back at 89A on the outskirts of West Sedona. Turn right and continue into town. Or go straight through the intersection onto Cultural Park Road where you'll find an unpaved parking area on your right. From this hilltop perch, enjoy sweeping views of the multihued cliffs that define the Sedona landscape. There's a shaded picnic ramada and a few benches. This is the trailhead for several pathways, including the Girdner Trail (see Hiking) and for the short gentle Centennial Trail, a 0.2-mile paved path through pinion pines to another overlook of mesas and mountains.

When you do continue into West Sedona, you'll find the heart of the community. The components of everyday life are here. Among the art galleries and hotels are grocery and hardware stores, movie theaters, a medical center, and library. This is where Sedona feels like a small town, not just a tourist destination. But a small town of indescribable beauty.

West Sedona is strung along the base of dome-shaped Capitol Butte. Coffee Pot Rock looms over neighborhoods looking real enough to flood the streets with steaming java. Airport Mesa rises above West Sedona. While only small aircraft use the facility, helicopter tours shuttle in and out throughout the day. The mesa top is also the most popular spot to watch a sunset, with crowds gathering every afternoon to cheer on the show.

Travel Note You'll find a few restaurants and shops in Cornville but don't expect fields of corn. The name was actually supposed to be Coneville, after an early settler, but somewhere along the way the spelling got altered on the paperwork.

More Scenic Driving

Extend your drive through wine country by turning right at the stoplight for Cornville Road as you leave Cottonwood. This will take you through the little burg of Cornville spread across lush bottomland. Turn left on Page Springs Road as it rambles through rural countryside in a series of winding curves that mimic the twists and turns of Oak Creek. Along the way you'll pass multiple vineyards and tasting rooms, including Page Springs Cellars, Oak Creek Vineyards, and Javelina Leap. Page Springs Fish Hatchery is directly across the road from the latter two and offers a nature trail, picnic tables, bird- watching, and a show pond where kids can feed the fish. Nearby Bubbling Ponds is an addition to the hatchery with a lovely 1.8-mile path through the trees and along the creek. Watch for river otters here. The drive is a total of 12 miles and rejoins 89A at the beginning of the official scenic road.

To explore some of Sedona's backcountry, turn left at Dry Creek Road in West Sedona off 89A (an actual street and not to be confused with Dry Creek Scenic Road). Follow it to a T intersection and turn left on Boynton Pass Road (FR 152C). At the next stop sign, a right turn leads to Enchantment Resort and the popular Boynton Canyon Trail. Hang a left and you'll continue past gorgeous formations and several more hiking options. Fay Canyon Trail is on the right, a forested walk with a view of an arch. The road continues past Bear Mountain, which is likely the most strenuous trail in Sedona. Just across the road is flat-topped Doe Mesa. The mile-long trail to the summit provides wraparound views of the countryside. Pavement ends but you can continue to ancient villages of the Sinagua people, Palatki and Honanki. Since visitation is limited, call (928) 282-3854 to make reservations for Palatki.

Hiking

SCORPION-PYRAMID LOOP

Starting from the guest parking lot of the Sedona High School, the Scorpion Trail hugs the flank of Schuerman Mountain winding through a pine and juniper woodland. (With hiking trails right outside the school's back door, why aren't more kids playing hooky?) The Pyramid Trail enters at the 1-mile mark. Continuing on Scorpion, you'll begin a gentle descent along rocky ledges until reconnecting to the Pyramid Trail. This stretch climbs onto a bench at the base of a towering wall of red sandstone. Keep an eye peeled for views of Cathedral Rock behind you that continue to change as you make a short but steep scramble onto the plateau. Follow the trail around to rejoin Scorpion and back to your vehicle for a 4.2-mile loop.

SKYWALKER TRAIL

Starting directly across the road from the same high school parking lot for Scorpion, the Skywalker Trail (1.8 miles) snakes its way across a plateau with views extending into all corners of red rock country. It makes a twisty ridge-hugging route over ground ablaze with wildflowers in the spring. Panoramas of some of Sedona's most iconic formations line both sides of the path. Skywalker ends at Old Post Trail, a former mail route back in horse-and-buggy days. Return the way you came or hang a right on Old Post for about a mile and then make another right on Herkenham Trail, which will return you to the trailhead in a 3.9-mile loop.

In a Christmas card come to life, Sedona's Thunder Mountain wears a picturesque mantle of snow. Courtesy of Mike Koopsen, Sedona.

GIRDNER TRAIL #162

From the Cultural Park Trailhead, the Girdner weaves through juniper groves with sweeping views for the first mile before making a gentle descent to Dry Creek. The route demands multiple crossings of this channel, so don't attempt after heavy rains. As the name implies, Dry Creek does little more than harbor the occasional pool or puddle. But it's enough to create a lovely riparian habitat. You'll stay in the shallow canyon bottom for a couple of miles, passing beneath a graceful canopy of sycamores. Scramble onto higher ground for vistas of a salmon-and-coral rockscape. The trail continues through desert woodlands before ending at Dry Creek Road in 4.5 miles.

Information for all hiking trails: (928) 203-2900, www.fs.usda.gov/coconino.

Where to Eat and Stay

CREMA CRAFT KITCHEN + BAR, COTTONWOOD

More than just a restaurant specializing in brunch items, Crema Craft Kitchen is a gathering spot, a flavorful hub in Old Town Cottonwood. The historic building houses the kitchen and a handful of tables while the bulk of the seating spills out into the colorful courtyard. This is where you'll find virtually everyone in the community as they linger over delicious plates of chicken and waffles, banana nutella crepes, chilaquiles, lobster salads, and more. 917 N. Main St., (928) 649-5785, www.cremacottonwood.com.

PISA LISA, SEDONA

This restaurant offers delicious wood-fired pizzas and gourmet salads in a stylish setting in West Sedona. The sauces and dressings were created at Chef Lisa Dahl's fine dining restaurants in town and add a decadent touch to this casual eatery. The pizza crust is thin but firm and beautifully charred. The Au Sauvage is topped with Calabrese sausage, prosciutto, picante peppers, spicy coppa, and soppressata salami. 2245 W. Arizona 89A, (928) 282-5472, www.pisalisa.com.

TAVERN HOTEL, COTTONWOOD

Offering upscale lodging, the Tavern Hotel is located in the heart of Old Town, just footsteps from several shops, restaurants, and wine-tasting rooms. Hardwood floors, granite countertops, stone-tiled bathrooms with walk-in showers, and plush bedding are all part of the contemporary feel for these well-appointed rooms. And taking advantage of their location, the Tavern also offers several packages in conjunction with local attractions—the most popular is the Sip and Stay Wine Package. 904 N. Main St., (928) 639-1669, www.thetavernhotel.com.

SEDONA ROUGE HOTEL AND SPA, SEDONA

This boutique hotel affords guests a surprisingly private getaway in a convenient urban location. Rooms are decorated in a Mediterranean style with bold, rich colors and plush fabrics. Expect some nice details like rain showers and gourmet coffee service. Some rooms have views, and there's an observation deck along with a heated pool. The on-site spa offers massages, stone therapy, and a special couple's treatment. While the design of the seventy-seven-room hotel provides maximum privacy, Sedona Rouge is in the middle of West Sedona, with plenty of stuff nearby. 2250 W. Arizona 89A, (928) 203-4111, www.sedonarouge.com.

When You Go

Cottonwood Chamber of Commerce: 849 Cove Parkway, (928) 634-7593, www.cottonwoodchamberaz.org.

The Red Rock All-American Road skirts past Bell Rock and Courthouse Butte. Courtesy of Mike Koopsen, Sedona.

Old Town Cottonwood: (928) 634-7593, www.oldtown.org.

Sedona Chamber of Commerce: 331 Forest Rd., (928) 282-7722, www.visitsedona.com.

Red Rock State Park: Fee. (928) 282-6907, www.azstateparks.com.

Crescent Moon Picnic Site: Fee. (928) 203-2900, www.fs.usda.gov/coconino.

Page Springs Cellars: 1500 N. Page Springs Rd., (928) 639-3004, www.pagespringscellars.com.

Oak Creek Vineyards & Winery: 1555 N. Page Springs Rd., (928) 649-0290, www.oakcreekvineyards.net.

Javelina Leap Vineyard & Winery: 1565 N. Page Springs Rd., (928) 649-2681, www.javelinaleapwinery.com.

Page Springs Hatchery: 1600 N. Page Springs Rd., (928) 634-4805.

Red Rock All-American Road

Overview This is one of two All-American Roads in the state, considered a destination unto itself. Arizona 179 exits from the interstate and makes a dramatic entrance to the red rock wonderland of Sedona.

Route Numbers Arizona State Highway 179.

Mileage The All-American Road is 7.5 miles (Milepost 302.5 to Milepost 310). It is 15 miles to Sedona from Interstate 17 at Exit 298.

Special Notes During holidays and busy weekends, increased traffic can cause congestion and make for slow going. Relax and enjoy the views. This road provides access to Dry Creek Scenic Road, and Sedona–Oak Creek Canyon Scenic Road.

Unless you're locked in the trunk of a car, there's no way to arrive in Sedona that doesn't steal your breath and pop your eyes wide. Every paved road into town is an

A summer monsoon rainbow highlights the Chapel of the Holy Cross. Courtesy of Mike Koopsen, Sedona.

official scenic road. If you've got a high-clearance vehicle, you could sneak in by bouncing down the rough and rutted Schnebly Hill Road, an old wagon route hacked from a mountainside. It lacks any scenic designation because of its primitive character but may actually be the most stunning of all.

Red Rock All-American Road is the magic carpet ride. This is the primary gateway to red rock country. Most Sedona visitors arrive via this road, streaming in from Phoenix, 110 miles to the south.

From Interstate 17, take Exit 298 onto Arizona 179. It appears first as just a winding country drive, curving through grasslands and a jumble of hills. But it's not long until red sandstone monoliths pop into view. Just a quick flash and then they're gone. Until suddenly they're not. It seems to happen almost all at once, and then all you can see is red, a wall of scandalous and passionate stone. If Eskimos have dozens of words for snow, Sedonans need just as many for the color red.

These are shades of fire engines, ripe strawberries, and Santa's pajamas. Scan the cliffs and you'll see valentines, cherries, sunsets, and rubies. They are reds from up and down the spectrum, bracketed by hues of orange and cream.

It's all because the rocks are rusty. Sedona formations contain hematite, a reddish form of iron oxide similar to rust. Water carrying dissolved iron oxide deposited the hematite as it seeped through layers of sandstone, the remnants of ancient dunes.

Your first stop should be the Red Rock Ranger District Visitor Center to grab maps, information, and permits. A Red Rock Pass is required to park at some trailheads and other recreation sites. They are available by the day, week, and year. A short film is shown in the theater on the hour and half hour. With more than 400 miles of hiking trails weaving among the formations, you'll have no shortage of options when it comes time to get out and walk around.

As you approach the Village of Oak Creek, Bell Rock, Courthouse Butte and

Castle Rock dominate the skyline. Nestled in the open expanse of Big Park, the Village was originally a bedroom community but now offers first-class lodging, restaurants, shops, the only eighteen-hole golf course open to the public in red rock country, and a great network of hiking and biking trails.

I always think of Bell Rock as Sedona's official greeter. The big dollop of stone perched at the edge of the road provides a stunning welcome and begs for a photo op. Fortunately, there's a large parking area in front (Bell Rock Vista) and another on the backside (Courthouse Vista) of the stone that resembles a brawny Hershey kiss. From both you can access the Bell Rock Pathway, a wide level path that's more thoroughfare than hiking trail for much of its 3.6 miles as it brushes past Bell and parallels the road. But it does serve as a launching pad for other trails that quickly leave the crowds behind, like Courthouse Butte Loop that throws a lasso around the big blocky neighbor of Bell Rock.

The road divides as it leaves the Village and swings past Bell Rock. Several years earlier the Arizona Department of Transportation plan to upgrade tourist-laden 179 was to build a traditional but invasive five-lane river of pavement, two lanes for each direction plus a turn lane. Residents were concerned that such a project would affect quality of life and damage the landscape. They worked with ADOT to achieve the current design, which was completed in 2010.

The bifurcated road includes a single lane moving in each direction, with a bike lane attached. The segments are separated by a wide buffer of forest land through rolling hills, completely apart from each other. So for several miles the drive feels private and personal. Of course, the downside of the aesthetically pleasing design is that with only a single lane flowing into Sedona, backups can occur during busy times.

The long line of cliffs to the right is part of the Munds Mountain Wilderness. Cathedral Rock looms on the left side of the highway looking different from every angle. Cathedral is also one of Sedona's famous vortex sites. Sedona vortexes (the proper grammatical form "vortices" is rarely used here) are thought to be swirling centers of energy that are conducive to spiritual healing, meditation, and self-exploration. Believers identify four primary vortexes. In addition to Cathedral, they're located at Bell Rock, Boynton Canyon, and Airport Mesa.

The officially designated scenic drive ends at Milepost 310, but the dazzling scenery continues as you enter a mix of residential and national forest land. To your right you'll spot one of Sedona's most compelling works of art, the Chapel of the Holy Cross. Turn right on Chapel Road for a closer look. Designed by sculptor Marguerite Staude, the chapel thrusts upward between two pillars of rock. High cliffs of salmon hues form the backdrop. The interior of the chapel is simple and unadorned. A few benches, some tapestries, and flickering candles create a serene, meditative oasis. Come for the sweeping views, or a little quiet contemplation, or both.

If the landscape seems eerily familiar, blame it on Hollywood. Over the decades, dozens of movies have been filmed in Sedona. Westerns were especially well represented, and many of the streets reflect that cinematic legacy with names like Flaming Arrow Way, Eagle Dancer Road, Johnny Guitar Street, Pony Soldier Road, and Last Wagon Drive.

As you approach the outskirts of Sedona, you'll pass a concentrated collection of art galleries and shops strung along the road. This is known as Gallery Row.

At Schnebly Hill Road, 179 makes a sharp left and crosses Oak Creek. Tlaquepaque Arts & Crafts Village sits along both sides of the road. The Spanish-style

Travel Note Rugged Schnebly Hill Road was named for T. C. Schnebly and his wife, who settled near here. The young couple often provided lodging and food for weary travelers along the rough wagon route. When T. C. became the first postmaster for the fledgling community, he offered a couple of suggestions for names but they were rejected for being too long. In the end, he simply named the town after his lovely wife, Sedona.

buildings are reminiscent of a Mexican hamlet. Cobblestone walkways meander past vine-covered walls and beneath stone archways. Graceful sycamore trees shade the courtyards where shoppers stroll past splashing fountains and beds bursting with flowers. Tlaquepaque houses assorted upscale galleries, shops, and restaurants.

Arizona 179 ends a couple of blocks later where it joins Arizona 89A, the other main artery through Sedona. The traffic circle where the two roads meet is known as the "Y" by locals. Most directions you might receive while in town will involve the "Y." Turn left to go to West Sedona and Cottonwood, or turn right to proceed to Uptown Sedona and on through Oak Creek Canyon.

More Scenic Driving

Schnebly Hill Road makes a twisted ascent through red rock tablelands to the pine forests just south of Flagstaff. While the first mile is paved, the road quickly turns

primitive—a lane pockmarked and ledged. Don't attempt this without a high-clearance vehicle. You'll climb in the shadow of big sandstone cliffs and curl around behind Merry-Go-Round Rock, a popular site for weddings. Panoramas widen the higher you go until finally topping out in the forests. The road turns smoother after that and dead ends at Interstate 17 (Exit 320) in Munds Park. To save wear and tear on your vehicle, nearly all Sedona jeep companies offer Schnebly Hill tours.

Hiking

BELL TRAIL #13

When exiting I-17, instead of turning west toward Sedona, turn east on FR 618 and follow the gravel road for 2 miles with signs guiding you to the trailhead. During summer months, most people hiking Bell Trail (not to be confused with Bell Rock Pathway) are bound for "The Crack" (3.3 miles), a legendary swimming hole. But no need to venture that far if you crave a personal oasis. Staying on a sunny bench above Wet Beaver Creek, the trail skirts the base of desert hills. Several well-used social paths branch off and lead to the stream at prime pools and smooth rock mini-beaches. Stroll down to the inviting shade of sycamores and cottonwoods draping the water. The stream is a sly beauty with a complex tune. The water runs fast and shallow—colliding with boulders, rushing through chutes—creating a splashy symphony around every bend.

LITTLE HORSE TRAIL #61

The trails starts out on Bell Rock Pathway before quickly branching off. It crosses a dry streambed and climbs gently into a bewitching woodland guarding the flanks of a stony plateau. You'll pass twin spires known as the Nuns and a signed path leading to the Chapel of the Holy Cross. At 1.5 miles, the trail clambers up onto a massive slickrock saddle surrounded by a panorama of eroded cliffs. The dramatic setting is called Chicken Point, but it's hard to figure out why. Maybe because it looks nothing like a chicken. But it makes a great place to soak in the sights. Don't expect an abundance of solitude, however. Chicken Point is a popular stop for jeep tours. If you want to hike further, continue on Broken Arrow Trail, which will lead to Submarine Rock and the sinkhole known as the Devils Dining Room. Trailhead is on the east side of

A blazing sunset streaks the sky above Cathedral Rock. Courtesy of Mike Koopsen, Sedona.

179 past Milepost 309. A Red Rock Pass is required, available at the trailhead kiosk.

SLIM SHADY–MADE IN THE SHADE LOOP

Slim Shady is a popular mountain biking route that parallels 179 and dishes up a rolling panorama of iconic formations. From Yavapai Vista, a web of short trails fan out but maps are posted at each junction. Follow the Kaibab Trail straight to Slim Shady. The curvy single track ambles at a slight downhill through pines and junipers on the flank of rocky hills. Views of Bell Rock and Courthouse Butte across the highway are exquisite. Pass the first junction with Made in the Shade, but hang a right at the second and begin to loop back. You'll make a gentle climb closer to the cliffs for more outstanding views. Along the way it crosses a couple of slickrock ledges that make primo seats for a picnic. Yavapai Vista Trailhead can only be accessed from the southbound lane of Arizona 179, 1.4 miles south of the Back O' Beyond traffic circle, which is at Milepost 310. A Red Rock Pass is required, available at the trailhead kiosk.

Information for all hiking trails: (928) 203-2900, www.fs.usda.gov/coconino.

Where to Eat and Stay

CUCINA RUSTICA, VILLAGE OF OAK CREEK

Resembling a romantic Tuscan villa with fireplaces and fountains, elaborate ironwork, and old-world doors, Cucina Rustica is perfect for special occasions like birthdays, anniversaries or any day ending in the letter "Y." The ambiance combined with the stealthy, ninja-like professionalism of the waitstaff and the rich Italian-inspired cuisine makes every occasion special. Their farm-to-table practice assures fresh seasonal flavors. Specialty desserts are whipped up nightly. 7000 Arizona 179, (928) 284-3010, www.cucinarustica.com.

ELOTE CAFÉ, SEDONA

No matter what else you order, start with the signature elote, fire-roasted corn fresh off the cob, lightly tossed with spicy mayo and cotija cheese. It's based on a common street food in Mexico, but Chef Jeff Smedstad gives it a devastatingly tasty spin. All the dishes reverberate with rich, complementary flavors. They're only open for dinner and if you don't arrive early, expect a wait. Fortunately, they also serve some of the best margaritas in town, which will help make the time pass. 350 Jordan Rd., (928) 203-0105, www.elotecafe.com.

INN ABOVE OAK CREEK, SEDONA

Sometimes a name tells you a lot about a place. The Inn Above Oak Creek delivers exactly what it promises. Perched above the water amid a grove of trees, the two-story inn features thirteen individually decorated rooms that include touches like gas fireplaces and whirlpool tubs. Guests enjoy the best of both worlds at the inn. Stroll down to the stream and enjoy a private oasis, or walk to dozens of shops, galleries, and restaurants in Tlaquepaque and Hillside Sedona. 556 Arizona 179, (928) 282-7896, www.innaboveoakcreek.com.

SEDONA HILLTOP INN, SEDONA

If you ever took a family road trip in a station wagon, you probably stayed at a place just like the Sedona Hilltop Inn. It's an older property but has been well maintained with bigger than average rooms. It sits in a sweet location, right between Tlaquepaque and the Shops at Pinon Pointe. Sip a glass of wine from the covered patio in the evening and watch the last rays of sun wash over Snoopy Rock. 218 Arizona 179, (928) 282-7187, www.thesedonamotel.com.

Munds Wagon Trail climbs into Sedona's signature red rock country. Courtesy of Mike Koopsen, Sedona.

When You Go

Red Rock Ranger District Visitor Center: 8375 Arizona 179, (928) 203-2900, www.fs.usda.gov/coconino.

Chapel of the Holy Cross: 780 Chapel Rd., (928) 282-7545, www.chapeloftheholycross.com.

Tlaquepaque Arts & Crafts Village: 336 Arizona 179, (928) 282-4838, www.tlaq.com.

Sedona Chamber of Commerce: 331 Forest Rd., (928) 282-7722, www.visitsedona.com.

Sedona–Oak Creek Canyon Scenic Road

Overview Traverse a spectacular canyon of colorful red cliffs and verdant forests while following the course of Oak Creek. The drive gains over 2,000 feet of elevation in a few short miles traveling from Sedona to Flagstaff on a road that frequently ends up on lists for most scenic drives in America.

Route Numbers Arizona State Highway 89A.

Mileage The scenic road is 14.5 miles (Milepost 375.5 to Milepost 390). It is 28 miles from Sedona to Flagstaff.

Special Notes Winter storms can force temporary closure of the road at the switchbacks in Oak Creek Canyon. This road provides access to Dry Creek

Scenic Road, Red Rock All-American Road, and San Francisco Peaks Scenic Road.

Perhaps more than any other feature, Arizona is defined by canyons. All across the state, those great gouges in the landscape harbor scenery and secrets. While the Grand Canyon leaves visitors awestruck and grasping for words, it's Oak Creek Canyon that steals their hearts and makes them ponder giving everything up to move to a cabin in the woods.

The sumptuous riparian defile connects the red rock wonderland of Sedona to the high ramparts of the Colorado Plateau where Flagstaff nestles amid a forest of ponderosa pines. And it all happens in a few short miles.

This highway also plays a significant role in my personal history with the state. I fell in love with Arizona as soon as I arrived in Flagstaff as a college student. But it was this road that first introduced me to the sheer staggering diversity of the landscape.

Flagstaff was having a snowy winter during my freshman year, and on one particularly blustery day a few friends piled into my roommate's car and went cruising off the mountain. We drove through pine forests and snaked our way down the switchbacks into Oak Creek Canyon. We followed the stream until somewhere near Sedona we stopped and piled out. There was no snow, no wind, and no chill. It was a gorgeous sunny day, at least 20 degrees warmer than the campus we left a half hour before.

It was a brand-new world among the red rock castles and towers of Sedona. We soaked up some sun and splashed in the creek literally thirty minutes from our snow-covered mountain. I was just beginning to comprehend the calculus of altering elevations. What a sweet bit of magic to be able to change worlds, to change seasons in a matter of minutes.

Travel Note Due to the faulting that played a role in the formation of Oak Creek Canyon, the western rim of the gorge is 700 feet higher than the eastern rim.

This sliver of road through the canyon began as a cattle trail then grew into a rough wagon route crossing the creek over and over again. As a highway—the northernmost segment of Arizona 89A—it is a doozy. This became the first state highway designated as a scenic road by the Arizona Department of Transportation in 1984.

The road heads north from Sedona, leaving the shops and galleries behind but maintaining the big vistas of sculpted formations. It parallels Oak Creek, staying well above the water at this point. After the first few curves, you'll cross Midgley Bridge. Dedicated in 1939, the 200-foot-long steel arch bridge spans Wilson Canyon. Take advantage of the small parking area to admire the impressive views of the structure and the surrounding scenery. This also serves as a trailhead for pathways such as Wilson Canyon Trail and Huckaby Trail (see Hiking).

A half-mile beyond the bridge is one of Oak Creek Canyon's great swimming holes, Grasshopper Point. Bracketed by small, feisty waterfalls and guarded by a clutch of graceful Arizona sycamores, the stream gathers in a blue green pool 50 feet wide at the base of a terraced cliff. Swimmers can make a straight plummet into deep water from varying heights.

There are several roadside pullouts as well as developed stops where you can marvel at the scenery and the feeling of being immersed in this oasis that combines craggy canyon walls and dense greenery, a rare crossroads of desert gauntness and lush abundance. Indian Gardens Café & Market nestles in a stretch of bottomland cradled by big sycamores. They sell supplies, gourmet sandwiches, and more with a lovely patio around back. This was the original homestead site in the area, as commemorated by a plaque across the road. In the 1870s, Jim Thompson—who obviously had a keen eye for real estate—became the first Anglo settler in the canyon.

Just a bit farther up the road sits the most idyllic Dairy Queen you'll likely find. How often do you get to enjoy a Blizzard with a side of awesome scenery? As a bonus, Native American vendors sell their jewelry and art from tables set up in the parking lot.

Seven miles north of Sedona, Slide Rock State Park occupies the site of another homestead. This one is complete with historic buildings and orchards growing in the shadow of rising red cliffs. They still produce apples that are sold by the sackful and made into cider during autumn. The park is open year-round and is packed during the summer as revelers take advantage of the natural waterslide formed when the stone banks squeeze the creek into a narrow channel. Deep pools and rock-ledge diving platforms add another element of watery play. If you're hoping to join the fun at this legendary swimming hole, try to go on a weekday and arrive early.

Picnic areas and campgrounds are scattered through the heart of the canyon as you continue to gain elevation. This is a mixed forest. Junipers and pines are intermingled with oaks, cottonwoods, sycamores, walnuts, box elders, maples, and ash. Come autumn, this menagerie puts on a vivid display reminiscent of a New England country drive. The perennial flow of water from the creek keeps the woods healthy and full, crowding the road in places supported by a dense understory. At times it feels like you're burrowing through a living tunnel of greenery.

Don't be surprised if the Call of the Canyon Picnic Site is packed with vehicles. More than just a few picnic tables, this is also the trailhead for famed West Fork Trail. The easy pathway is often rated as one of the most scenic hikes in Arizona and in a state with the Grand Canyon, Monument Valley, and plenty of other heavyweights, that's high praise indeed. The path traces a gentle stream into a narrow defile framed by soaring, scandalously hued sandstone cliffs. It's a mesmerizing combination of soft forest and sheer stone, intimacy and dizzying drama. The maintained trail is 3.3 miles and includes 13 creek crossings, so a sturdy walking stick makes a welcome companion. Operated by a concessionaire, this is a fee site.

After passing a couple of final campgrounds and crossing Pumphouse Wash, the switchbacks begin. These are a series of tight hairpin curves rising sharply up through the forest, seeming to climb the canyon wall. It finally tops out on the forested plateau with the turnout for Oak Creek Canyon Vista. Here you'll find restrooms, a visitor information stand, and Native American vendors. But all that will have to wait a few minutes while you walk to the edge and savor the epic panorama.

It's amazing to see the savage cleft of Oak Creek Canyon spread out below you—although not as cool as driving through it. The road continues for the next several miles through the ponderosa pines to Flagstaff.

Travel Note While staying in cabins at the head of West Fork, Western writer Zane Grey penned *Call of the Canyon*. It was to become the first of his novels turned into a movie. At Grey's insistence, the filmmakers shot the 1923 silent Western on location just where it was written.

Hiking

BRINS MESA TRAIL #119

Towering red cliffs loom above the parking area not far from Uptown Sedona, so the stunning views start before you're out of the car and never let up. The first portion of the hike rambles across a landscape shaggy with cypress before reaching the foot of the mesa. Formations peep through at every opening. The climb to the top is a moderate slog, but each time you pause to catch your breath, you'll be rewarded by an expanding scenic tableau. Cresting the ridge at 1.5 miles, you'll be gazing at the rising walls of Red Rock Secret Mountain Wilderness and beyond. The trail slices across the broad back of Brins Mesa before ending at Vultee Arch Road after 3 miles.

HUCKABY TRAIL #161

You can access the Huckaby from Midgley Bridge, but since parking is limited, consider the other trailhead, a mile up Schnebly Hill Road, before the pavement ends. From here, the first half of the trail crosses Bear Wallow Wash and climbs an exposed mesa overlooking Sedona. After a mile, the trail curves around Mitten Ridge displaying views of Steamboat Rock and Wilson Mountain. The ribbon of Oak Creek is visible a few hundred feet below. It's a gentle descent into shady woodlands. The Huckaby arrives at the creek amid a tangle of trees and rising canyon walls. Enjoy this peaceful little spot before turning around for a four-mile round-trip hike. Or cross the creek twice (tricky if the water is running high) and then follow the switchbacks up to the bridge, which will add just over a mile to your outing. A Red Rock Pass is required, available at the trailhead kiosk.

Autumn colors are a highlight of West Fork Trail in Oak Creek Canyon. Courtesy of Mike Koopsen, Sedona.

MUNDS WAGON TRAIL #78

From the same Schnebly Hill parking area as Huckaby, Munds Wagon Trail heads east up Bear Wallow Canyon. It parallels Schnebly Hill Road and the views are striking right from the start. The trail stays level early on and crosses the road a couple of times before descending through a grove of Arizona cypress to a shallow drainage. Water flow is sporadic but you can usually find small pools, including some lined by cattails. The trail junctions with Cow Pies Trail just after 2 miles, and this makes a good turnaround point. Better still, you can include the Pies in your hiking itinerary. It's only a half-mile trail out to the big sandstone platforms known as Cow Pies, where you'll enjoy fantastic views back down the canyon you just traveled. A Red Rock Pass is required, available at the trailhead kiosk.

Information for all hiking trails: (928) 203-2900, www.fs.usda.gov/coconino.

Where to Eat and Stay

SEDONA MEMORIES BAKERY & CAFÉ, SEDONA

If you're looking to put together a picnic lunch to enjoy in Oak Creek Canyon, load up at Sedona Memories Bakery & Café. Tucked away just off the main drag in Uptown Sedona, this family-owned sandwich shop is a favorite of locals and savvy tourists. Quality ingredients are piled on homemade bread to such staggering heights, each sandwich should require a building permit. Sedona Memories also serves soups, salads, pastries, and homemade cookies. But don't dawdle—they're only open till 2:00 p.m. Cash only. 321 Jordan Rd., (928) 282-0032.

TOURIST HOME ALL DAY CAFÉ, FLAGSTAFF

A decrepit former boardinghouse for Basque sheepherders in Flagstaff was saved from the wrecking ball and beautifully restored. Inside it's bright and cheerful with a few retail items and counter seating. Located in Flag's Southside, Tourist Home serves a fresh simple menu with a brunchy feel. They're especially known for packed breakfast burritos and an array of colorful pastries. 52 S. San Francisco St., (928) 779-2811, www.touristhomecafe.com.

BUTTERFLY GARDEN INN, OAK CREEK CANYON

Deep in Oak Creek Canyon, Butterfly Garden Inn offers twenty cozy rustic cabins spread across well-tended grounds. They range in size from three-bedroom family units with full kitchens to single cabins. Enjoy a quiet getaway in the shady canyon close to the flowing creek. Cabins don't come with televisions, but DVD players with TVs can be rented. A market and café are also on the premises. 9440 N. Arizona 89A, (928) 203-7633, www.thebutterfly gardeninn.com.

STARLIGHT PINES BED AND BREAKFAST, FLAGSTAFF

Nestled at the foot of Mt. Elden in East Flagstaff, Starlight Pines practically defines the bed-and-breakfast experience. Oak plank floors run throughout the spacious Victorian home. Four exquisite rooms are filled with antiques, claw-foot bathtubs, Tiffany lamps, fainting couches, wood-burning fireplaces, and other romantic touches. A 70-foot wraparound porch with a swing is delightful and should be mandatory at all inns. A gourmet breakfast is served daily. 3380 E. Lockett Rd., (928) 527-1912, www.starlightpinesbb.com.

When You Go

Sedona Chamber of Commerce: 331 Forest Rd., (928) 282-7722, www.visitsedona.com.

Indian Gardens Café & Market: 3951 N. Arizona 89A, (928) 282-7702, www.indiangardens.com.

Slide Rock State Park: Fee. (928) 282-3034, www.azstateparks.com.

Flagstaff Convention and Visitors Bureau: 1 E. Route 66, (928) 213-2951, www.flagstaffarizona.org.

NORTHERN ARIZONA

San Francisco Peaks Scenic Road

Overview Passing through thick forests, mountain meadows, and sagebrush flats, this road travels along the edge of Arizona's tallest mountains and provides one of the primary routes to Grand Canyon.

Route Numbers US Highway 180.

Mileage The scenic road is 31 miles (Milepost 224 to Milepost 255). It's 74 miles from Flagstaff to Grand Canyon National Park.

Special Notes Winter weather conditions apply, but since this road leads to downhill and cross-country skiing, that probably doesn't come as a shock. Carry chains, a shovel, and warm clothes. This road provides access to Sedona–Oak Creek Canyon Scenic Road and Historic Route 66 All-American Road (Ash Fork to Lupton).

We all cherish the memory of our first love.

For me, it was Flagstaff. That's where I first set foot in Arizona. I flew across the country from my Ohio home to attend college at Northern Arizona University. On a late summer's evening I stepped off a tiny plane (pretty sure we dusted crops on the final leg from Denver) and smelled the pine-scented air of Flagstaff. The next morning I saw the outline of the San Francisco Peaks. It was love at first sight.

I was utterly smitten with the mountains. I couldn't get enough of them and knew I was destined to be some kind of flannel-shirted mountain man romping at high elevation where the air is clean and pure.

So imagine my shock when I eventually fell under the spell of harsh sun-blasted lands filled with cacti and rattlesnakes. I'm not sure what utter collapse of judgment, what failure of common sense led me down the reckless path to become a desert rat, but such is my fate. But no matter how much time I spend sweating among the saguaros, Flagstaff always holds a special place in my heart.

You can expect an impressive display of diversity on a road that travels from Arizona's highest mountains to its deepest canyon. And don't let the tall pine trees and meadows streaked with wildflowers fool you. Lurking beneath the soft façade is an explosive lava-spewing geological hotspot.

The San Francisco volcanic field spreads for 1,800 square miles across the southern quadrant of the Colorado Plateau, with the first eruptions occurring six million years ago. Even the mountains the road skirts around, the San Francisco Peaks, are the ragged remnants of a hulking stratovolcano. Geologists believe it once reached a height of 16,000 feet but continued to blast itself apart with repeated eruptions.

The four major summits of the San Francisco Peaks are Fremont, Doyle, Agassiz, and Humphreys. At 12,633 feet, Humphreys Peak is the highest point in Arizona and also where you'll find the only alpine tundra in the state. Traveling between these high lonely slopes across the plateau and into the arid depths of the nearby Grand Canyon was where biologist C. Hart Merriam developed his "life zones" concept—that altitude and temperature largely determine what type of plants grow in a particular place. While widely accepted today, it was a controversial notion when he published his findings in 1890.

The San Francisco Peaks have considerable religious significance for several American Indian tribes. The Hopis believe their Kachina gods dwell within the mountains, and they are one of four sacred mountains to the Navajos forming the boundaries of their homeland.

The moods of Grand Canyon are ever changing. Courtesy of Mike Koopsen, Sedona.

Travel Note The youngest volcano in the region is Sunset Crater, north of Flagstaff. It erupted one thousand years ago.

US 180 leaves from downtown Flagstaff and angles northwest along the western slope of the Peaks, as they're known locally. On the outskirts of town, you'll pass a couple of excellent museums. Housed in a building of volcanic rock, the Pioneer Museum covers a wide range of the region's past. Exhibits highlight a history of logging, ranching, and transportation. There are also displays on early medicine, which is fitting since this structure was Coconino County's first hospital for the poor. Look for the steam locomotive parked out front. The Museum of Northern Arizona tells the history of the Colorado Plateau, from its geologic creation to the peoples who have populated it. Since this scenic drive travels between two of the defining features of that vast uplift, a stop here will prove most insightful.

Watch for the turnoff to the Arizona Snowbowl 7 miles northwest of Flagstaff. Snowbowl Road (FR 516) makes a winding climb up the slopes for 8 miles to one of the major ski areas in the state. The Snowbowl offers multiple runs during the winter and a scenic chairlift ride to 11,500 feet during warmer months. There are several hiking trails along this road as well, including the trek to the top of Humphreys Peak. Starting from the Snowbowl parking area, the steep, challenging hike is just under 10 miles round trip. The last stretch is a lung-squeezing slog across exposed treeless tundra that should not be attempted if lightning is even a remote possibility.

For those that prefer their skiing on more level terrain, Arizona Nordic Village offers miles of groomed cross-country trails during the winter, and cabins and yurts for

Downtown Flagstaff is filled with historic buildings and is known for its shops, restaurants, bars, and microbreweries. Photo by the author.

rent throughout the year. Look for it on the right side of 180, a couple of miles past the Snowbowl Road.

As the road continues, evidence of past fires are visible as well as the regeneration process. As you enter the wide grasslands of Kendrick Park, glance up the slopes of the peaks and you'll see the shimmering green of fast-growing aspen saplings filling the place where ponderosa pines once stood. Meadows spread out wide through here, a good area to spot wildlife. To the west, Kendrick Mountain, a large lava dome, rises above the forest.

The road begins to descend and the stately ponderosas give way to a scrubby mix of junipers and pinion pines. Red Mountain looms to the left, a volcanic cinder cone. Basically just assume every hill and mountain you see along this road were volcanoes or mixed up in volcanic treachery. And they may not be finished. Many geologists expect eruptions again in the future. I'm not sure how you would prepare for such an event if it happens during your scenic road trip other than to exercise caution. Do not try to cross a wash flowing with lava. And if hot magma is raining down from the sky, put the top up on the convertible and turn around at the first opportunity.

Red Mountain still wears visible scars of its violent past. It appears to have its side ripped out, exposing a fancifully eroded internal structure that you can enter (see Hiking).

For the last stretch of highway, you're clear of the forest and rolling across sagebrush prairie. After 50 miles you'll junction with Arizona 64 in the crossroads town of Valle. If you have time, one worthwhile stop is the Planes of Fame Air Museum where a cavernous hangar is filled to the rafters with restored antique planes, warbirds, models, munitions, equipment, and even a few classic cars.

Since you likely didn't come all this way to hang out in Valle, turn north on Arizona 64 to continue to Grand Canyon National Park. It's only 25 miles to the park entrance. Open country continues until the road climbs back into the forest before it reaches the town of Tusayan, just outside the park.

Please don't be the person who only spends two hours at Grand Canyon. Plan ahead so you can visit for a day, or several of them. If it is your first time, stop at the visitor center to get oriented. You can walk to Mather Point from there, an amazing viewpoint.

You can leave the car parked and take free shuttle buses everywhere. But if your schedule is really tight, decide how much time you want to spend in a vehicle of any kind. Consider just taking a long walk on the Rim Trail to maximize your canyon connection.

The Rim Trail does just as it promises, stretching for 13 miles along the edge of this natural wonder. It's mostly level, mostly paved (dirt only at the far ends), and shaded—and the views are relentless. It stretches from Yaki Point west all the way to Hermits Rest, passing Mather Point and through Grand Canyon Village, where you'll find shops, restaurants, hotels, and cabins. Use the shuttle bus to catch a ride back if you get tired.

More Scenic Driving

When your time is finished at Grand Canyon, exit via the Desert View Drive, a continuation of Arizona 64. The road turns east as it approaches the visitor center and travels for 25 miles through the forests along the edge of the South Rim. Far from the crowds of Grand Canyon Village, the road provides quiet moments with the canyon and an opportunity to encounter wildlife. Stop at the multiple pullouts and iconic overlooks for magnificent panoramas—Grandview Point, Moran Point, and Lipan Point are all stunning. But they save the best for last. At the far eastern edge of the park, Desert View offers services like a general store and deli, gift shop, gas station, and seasonal campground. Perched on the rim of the canyon is the Watchtower, a 70-foot stone tower designed by architect Mary Colter. Slender curving stairways climb to the top, where visitors enjoy rapturous views from the observation deck of the exposed strata and river below. As the road exits the park, it continues along the Little Colorado River Gorge, finally ending at the town of Cameron. Turn right on US 89 and return to Flagstaff.

If you want a closer look at the San Francisco Peaks, a network of forest roads form a long loop around the old volcano. It's a great summer outing and popular in autumn (usually the first two weeks of October) when the aspens are ablaze with color. These are mostly unpaved roads but are generally in good condition. Traveling northwest from Flagstaff on US 180, turn right on FR 151 near Milepost 235. Follow

The San Francisco Peaks—the tallest mountains in the state—rise above Flagstaff. Courtesy of Mike Koopsen, Sedona.

151 for 1.6 miles to FR 418. Head east onto 418 as it winds through aspen groves and flows along the edge of the Kachina Peaks Wilderness. You'll see some burn scars from the Schultz Fire as you curve around the northeast side of the Peaks. After 11 miles you'll reach a T-junction with FR 552. Here you've got some options. A right turn on 552 will lead you to Lockett Meadow and a left turn will quickly connect with US 89 where you can ride the pavement back to Flagstaff. Or if you're enjoying the bouncy solitude of a dirt road, continue straight ahead until you encounter FR 420 (Schultz Pass Road) and follow it until it ends at US 180. Always check road conditions before setting out on a backcountry adventure. (928) 526-0866, www.fs.usda.gov/coconino.

Hiking

KENDRICK PARK WATCHABLE WILDLIFE TRAIL

This gentle loop moves from pine forest through open grassland. Between the two habitats, you may encounter a variety of bird and animal life. There are two options, a 0.25-mile paved loop suitable for wheelchairs or the longer 1.5-mile loop that pushes deeper into the woods past an aspen grove and returns along the edge of a lanky meadow. Move quietly and stay alert for mule deer, elk, pronghorn antelope, coyote, badger, and porcupine. Flitting among the branches are Steller's jay, Northern flicker, pygmy nuthatch, and more. Look for the signed parking area on the west side of 180, 7 miles past the turnoff for the Snowbowl.

LAVA RIVER CAVE

Explore one of the most unusual volcanic scars of the area when hiking a nearly mile-long lava tube hidden beneath the ponderosa pines. The cave was formed 700,000 years ago by a river of molten lava blasted from a volcanic vent in nearby Hart Prairie. The entrance requires a bit of scrambling over boulders but then the chamber widens. There are some tight spots, but the ceiling often soars dozens of feet overhead. At the Y, bear left. Dress warmly and carry at least two sources of light. Drive 9 miles north of Flagstaff on US 180 and turn left on Forest Road 245 (at Milepost 230). Continue 3 miles and turn left on FR 171. Drive for 1 mile and turn left on FR 171B to the parking lot.

RED MOUNTAIN TRAIL #159

With Grand Canyon beckoning just up the highway, most folks breeze past Red Mountain with barely a glance. Those that stop and make the hike (a 3-mile round trip) are rewarded with an intimate but otherworldly experience. The trail starts along an old road that winds through junipers and pinion pines, then dips into the bed of a wash. After a mile the sandy streambed squeezes between towers of black cinders. A ladder climbs over a stone wall, and you're engulfed in a wonderland of gnawed spires, twisted pillars, and contorted walls bubbled with trapped gasses. The amphitheater calls to mind a miniaturized Bryce Canyon bristling with colorful hoodoos. Trail begins at Milepost 247 off US 180, 25 miles northwest of Flagstaff.

Information for all hiking trails: (928) 526-0866, www.fs.usda.gov/coconino.

Where to Eat and Stay

CRIOLLO LATIN KITCHEN, FLAGSTAFF

Although the cuisine of this downtown Flagstaff eatery originates in distant lands, the makings mostly come from the 'hood. Criollo specializes in Latin-inspired dishes but utilizes local, organic, and sustainably

Desert View Watchtower perches at the eastern edge of Grand Canyon National Park. Courtesy of Mike Koopsen, Sedona.

grown ingredients. Every meal has a special charm, but the place really comes alive for their Happy Hour, when sliders, tacos, and empanadas pair with an extensive selection of local craft beers and wines. 16 N. San Francisco St., (928) 774-0541, www.criollo latinkitchen.com.

MARTANNE'S BURRITO PALACE, FLAGSTAFF

This little downtown eatery is an institution in this college town, renowned for their piled-high chilaquiles full of spice and crunch. Their buckwheat pancakes also have a devoted following. While MartAnne's made their reputation as a breakfast place, they expanded hours to include dinner filled with creative Mexican dishes. 112 E. Route 66, (928) 773-4701, www.martannes .com.

EL TOVAR DINING ROOM, GRAND CANYON

Whether you're hiking deep into the Grand Canyon or just gazing at it, you can work up quite an appetite. And there's no better place to satisfy it than at the historic El Tovar Hotel, perched right on the rim. Built in 1905 as a famed Harvey House, El Tovar is wrapped in native stone and dark Oregon pine offering the nicest rooms at the canyon. The menu is infused with subtle Southwestern influence. To avoid lunchtime crowds, try to be seated before the Grand Canyon Railway arrives at 11:45 a.m. (928) 638-2631, www.grandcanyonlodges .com.

LITTLE AMERICA, FLAGSTAFF

Set amid a five-hundred-acre forest, Little America makes for a relaxing getaway. The large rooms and suites are spread across multiple buildings. The spacious grounds include nature trails, gardens, pool, and a playground. During the holiday season, Little America puts on a dazzling light display and is home to the North Pole Experience, where kids get to visit Santa's workshop. 2515 E. Butler Ave., (928) 779-7900, flagstaff littleamerica.com.

When You Go

Flagstaff Convention and Visitors Bureau: 1 E. Route 66, (928) 213-2951, www.flag staffarizona.org.

Pioneer Museum: Fee. 2340 N. Fort Valley Rd., (928) 774-6272, www.arizona historicalsociety.org.

Museum of Northern Arizona: Fee. 3101 Fort Valley Rd., (928) 774-5213, www.musnaz .org.

Arizona Snowbowl: Fee. (928)779-1951, www.snowbowl.ski.

Arizona Nordic Village: Fee. (928)220-0550, www.arizonanordicvillage.com.

Planes of Fame Air Museum: Fee. (928) 635-1000, www.planesoffame.org.

Grand Canyon Chamber and Visitors Bureau: (844) 638-2901, grandcanyoncvb .org.

Grand Canyon National Park: Fee. (928) 638-7888, www.nps.gov/grca.

Fredonia–Vermilion Cliffs Scenic Road

Overview Snaking a course through a land that feels decidedly ancient, where birds the size of baby pterodactyls glide overhead, this road probes the vastness of the Arizona Strip—that sparsely populated swath of state cut off by the Grand Canyon.

Route Numbers US Highway 89A.

Mileage The scenic road is 82 miles (Milepost 525 to Milepost 607). It is 111 miles from Page to Fredonia.

Special Notes Anyone traveling to the North Rim of the Grand Canyon (Kaibab Plateau–North Rim National Scenic Byway) must travel this road. Expect severe winter weather atop the Kaibab Plateau. During winter months, the North Rim of Grand Canyon is closed due to snow.

Welcome to Arizona's loneliest landscape.

This is the place gregarious people have nightmares about. Sweeping plains, broad plateaus, and towering cliffs wrapped in sunset hues are all cut off from the rest of

US 89A flows along the base of the Vermilion Cliffs. Courtesy of Mike Koopsen, Sedona.

Travel Note In 1993, US 89 and US 89A were decommissioned as federal roads between Nogales and Flagstaff because interstate highways now covered that distance. Thus some of the other roads featured in this book—Mingus Mountain, Jerome-Clarkdale-Cottonwood, Dry Creek, and Sedona-Oak Creek Canyon—are all part of Arizona 89A, while this northern drive remains US 89A.

the state by the cosmic razor slash of the Grand Canyon. This is the Arizona Strip, and it makes the proverbial Middle of Nowhere look like Times Square.

Solitude casts a wide net here. Quiet is the coin of the realm and the horizon is your closest neighbor. This is where you come to hole up, hide out, or lose track of time. And it's the Fredonia–Vermilion Cliffs Scenic Road that slices across the vast emptiness and comes out the other side.

I'll say something here that even I find startling. I think this is my favorite drive in the state.

There may be others that are more scenic, certainly plenty that are more accessible. I have roads that I travel frequently to places that I care about more. Yet this is the road that haunts me. It's the one I return to over and over in my mind when stress piles up at my door and I yearn to disappear.

Officially, the scenic road begins at the small Navajo community of Bitter Springs, about 25 miles south of Page off US 89. It rambles north along the edge of the Echo Cliffs to Marble Canyon and crosses the Navajo Bridge.

When Navajo Bridge was completed in 1929, it was the highest steel arch bridge in the world. In 1995 the original bridge was

Travel Note Brought back from the brink of extinction by a captive breeding program, the California condor is the largest flying land bird in North America with a 9-foot wingspan.

replaced by one similar in design just downstream, and now the twin spans stretch across the yawning steep-sided gorge. The old bridge is open only to pedestrians and provides stunning views of the Colorado River 467 feet below. It's also a great spot to watch California condors that were reintroduced to the area in 1996. The Navajo Bridge Interpretive Center acts as the quasi-official visitor center for the area, so stop in to collect maps and information.

After crossing the bridge, you'll see the signed turnoff to Lees Ferry. The 5-mile road winds down through sloping hills to a rare spot. This is the only place through hundreds of miles of canyon country where a wagon could reach the Colorado River and a crossing could be managed.

Mormon leaders established a ferry at the remote outpost to offer transportation between Utah and Arizona Territory. John D. Lee was the first ferryman, settling here with some of his wives in 1872. For decades, people and animals were carried across the river in small boats. It was risky business. Boats capsized and plenty of folks drowned, but it was the only game in town.

Today Lees Ferry, part of the Glen Canyon National Recreation Area, is best known as the put-in place for Grand Canyon rafting trips and is a popular spot for fly fishermen. Although not participating in either activity, I am drawn to this sun-blasted bit of outback near the confluence of the Colorado and Paria Rivers. I show up in the bone-wilting summer heat without an agenda. I just come to enjoy the intermingled beauty and history. A trail leads along the river past stone buildings, the crumbling remains of a Mormon fort, and rusted equipment (see Hiking).

My favorite part of Lees Ferry sits back from the river. The Lonely Dell Ranch was

Historic Navajo Bridge serves as a pedestrian walkway so travelers can enjoy river views, while traffic crosses the newer span. Courtesy of Mike Koopsen, Sedona

Lonely Dell Ranch was homesteaded by Mormon pioneer John Lee, who started a ferry service across the Colorado River. Courtesy of Mike Koopsen, Sedona.

originally homesteaded by John Lee and later occupied by all the families that operated the ferry. To survive in this wilderness they needed to be self-sufficient and grow food for themselves and their animals. Extensive irrigation systems gave the barren desert a makeover. This unexpected oasis is preserved today by the National Park Service.

Tucked away at the base of colorful cliffs, big shade trees provide a cooling canopy for the ranch house and surrounding log cabins. An orchard spreads out from the yard. Birds flit among the tree branches, and their cheerful songs are only occasionally interrupted by the shrill buzz of a cicada, those mini-motors of summer. I pull up a hunk of shade and treat myself to a leisurely lunch in this civilized wilderness.

Back on 89A, the road bends southwest and you'll pass three small sanctuaries. Marble Canyon Lodge, Lees Ferry Lodge, and Cliff Dwellers Lodge all offer food, drink and shelter. They're spread a few miles apart as the road streaks along the base of the Vermilion Cliffs. What's the point of having a hideout if you can't eat and enjoy a cold beverage in the evening as the sun swabs the tall stone with a luscious creamy light?

The sheer escarpment of the Vermilion Cliffs runs for over 30 miles, from Lees Ferry west through House Rock Valley. The massive wall reaches heights of nearly 3,000 feet, a fractured upheaval, banded in an array of colors. This snarling vertical thrust forms the southern edge of Vermilion Cliffs National Monument. Established in 2000, the monument remains one of the most remote, isolated corners of the state. Hidden away amid the stark expanse are diverse landscapes such as the sculpted beauty of Coyote Buttes, White Pocket, and the Wave, as well as the carved defiles of Buckskin Gulch and Paria Canyon.

With tall cliffs lining the north side of the road, the broad sagebrush plains of House Rock Valley stretch to the south. About 20 miles west of Navajo Bridge you'll spot a historic marker. It commemorates a campsite of the 1776 Dominguez–Escalante Expedition. The Spanish missionary-explorers set out from Santa Fe seeking a northern route to California. They never made it, instead forging a 2,000-mile rambling circle through the Four Corners region before being turned back by weather and other hardships. Although the expedition did not fulfill their quest, their maps and journals would prove invaluable to later travelers.

Near the base of the Kaibab Plateau, the road brushes past a couple of picturesque but forlorn ranches. It's a hardy breed of folk who scratch out a living on the Strip. One swooping curve later and US 89A begins climbing a long slope. The Kaibab Plateau resulted from a folding of the earth's crust. Rock layers buckled and left behind a great hump of land. "Kaibab" is a Paiute Indian word meaning "mountain lying down," and that sums it up pretty well.

Richly scented conifer forests and soft

A hiker enjoys a beautiful day at the Wave. Courtesy of Mike Koopsen, Sedona.

green meadows are spread across the plateau. Just about the time you're sure that you're all alone atop this napping mountain, you'll reach the little crossroads burg of Jacob Lake. It sits at the junction of Arizona 67, the road that leads to the North Rim of the Grand Canyon, which is a pretty nice detour if you have the time. The entire commercial district of the town consists of Jacob Lake Inn, operating a motel with cabins, gas station, general store, restaurant, and bakery.

Travel Note The Wave, an exotic sandstone bowl laced with ribbons of swirling strata, has become a popular destination in recent years. Permits are required and extremely difficult to come by. To protect the delicate sandstone structure, the Bureau of Land Management limits access to only twenty people per day. Of those, ten are chosen in an online lottery four months in advance and the other ten are reserved for walk-ins, held at the field office in Kanab, Utah.

Keep an eye peeled for wildlife as you continue across the broad back of the plateau. The habitat supports a healthy population ranging from black bear to wild turkeys to the Kaibab squirrel. A subspecies of the Abert's squirrel, the tuft-eared white-tailed Kaibab squirrel exists nowhere else. Glimpses of the valley framed by red cliffs beyond begin appearing through breaks in the timber. The Le Fevre Scenic Overlook allows you a chance to pull over and see what's ahead. From there the road starts winding down the long hillside and onto the sagebrush prairie. It's back to the wide-open spaces again, much like on the other side of the plateau.

Just before reaching the town of Fredonia, you'll pass the turnoff for Arizona 389. Make a side trip to Pipe Spring National Monument, offering an unblinking look at American Indian and pioneer life in the

An angler tries his luck at Lees Ferry. Courtesy of Mike Koopsen, Sedona.

Old West. Built in 1870, the Mormon fort sheltered a rare water source amid the grasslands. Buildings have been restored, gardens have been replanted, and ranger-led tours are offered of Winsor Castle, the centerpiece structure of the property. Pipe Spring is located 15 miles west of Fredonia on Arizona 389.

Fredonia includes basic services and the Red Pueblo Museum, housing a surprising collection of Indian artifacts is a must stop. And while the scenic road and the state of Arizona ends here, it's certainly worth continuing the 7 miles north to Kanab, Utah. The town is loaded with charm where you'll find tree-lined streets, motels, restaurants, shops, and a long Hollywood history. Kanab feels like a virtual metropolis after the lonely drive just completed.

Travel Note Kanab made its screen debut in 1924 when Tom Mix and Tony the Wonder Horse filmed *Deadwood Coach*. Since then nearly 150 movies and television series have used the dramatic backdrop as a shooting location, and a parade of stars have passed through town.

Hiking

RIVER TRAIL

Starting at the launch ramp at Lees Ferry, the trail follows an old wagon road past a series of stone buildings in varying states of decline. The 1-mile path provides a look at the history of the ferry, as well as panoramas of riverside cliffs. The fort was built in 1874 during escalating tensions between the Navajos and Mormons. It was never attacked and later used as a trading post. Along with rusty pieces of equipment, you'll also see the wreck of a stern-wheel steamboat submerged in shallow water. The trail ends at the site of the old ferry, marked by pieces of cable and the crumbling foundations of rock houses. Fishermen's paths continue upstream.

CATHEDRAL WASH

Travel down a storm-carved arroyo with interesting rock formations to the river. After turning off US 89A onto Lees Ferry Road, drive 1.3 miles. Trailhead is at the pullout on your left. This is a moderate hike (1.25 miles) that involves scrambling, traversing ledges, and climbing up and down heights of 30 feet. The trail ends at picturesque Cathedral Wash Rapid on the Colorado River. Don't enter the wash during inclement weather due to the danger of flash flooding.

PARIA RIVER TRAIL

Starting from the Lonely Dell Ranch parking area, follow the path upstream along the Paria River and continue for as long as you like. Paria Canyon stretches for 45 miles into Utah and the hike through is a great backpacking expedition. Overnight hikes require a permit from the Bureau of Land Management. Day hikers can go as long as they like. Some wading may be necessary in the shallow river.

Information for all hiking trails: (928) 608-6200, www.nps.gov/glca.

Where to Eat and Stay

MARBLE CANYON LODGE

Sitting at the turnoff for Lees Ferry, Marble Canyon Lodge includes a motel, gas station, convenience store, trading post, and private airstrip. The restaurant serves American cuisine with a Southwestern flair. The motel was rebuilt following a fire in 2014, but the rooms retain their vintage charm. Many feature window views of the cliffs. They also offer apartments for larger groups. (928) 355-2225, www.marblecanyoncompany.com.

LEES FERRY LODGE AT VERMILION CLIFFS

Tucked against the towering sandstone cliffs 3 miles west of the turnoff for Lees Ferry, this rustic inn offers a restaurant and bar with an amazing beer selection. Even better, they've got one of the all-time great front porches. Everything just tastes better when consumed on a porch with a view. The motel is cozy with different configurations in each of their ten rooms. (928) 355-2231, www.vermilioncliffs.com.

CLIFF DWELLERS LODGE

You'll find another excellent porch at the restaurant at Cliff Dwellers along with tasty well-prepared food, including an amazing burger. Even something simple like chicken tenders come just the way you want them—a nice crunch on the outside, moist and succulent inside. Accommodations include some small vintage rooms with carports dating back to the 1950s along with a newer wing. The small market sells gas, and the fly shop is fully stocked with gear, tackle, and clothing. They also offer kayak rentals and shuttle service for anyone that would like to explore the stretch of Colorado River (all flat water) between Glen Canyon Dam and Lees Ferry. (928) 355-2261, www.cliffdwellerslodge.com.

AIKEN'S LODGE, KANAB

This mid-century classic motel is stylish, spotlessly clean, and sitting right in the heart of town. Rooms may be a bit on the smallish side, but you'll love the friendly staff and reasonable rates. There's also a pool and adjoining patio creating an old-school family-friendly environment. 79 W. Center, (435) 644-2625, www.aikenslodge.com.

When You Go

Navajo Bridge Interpretive Center: (928) 355-2319.
Lees Ferry: Fee. (928) 608-6200, www.nps.gov/glca.
Jacob Lake Inn: (928) 643-7232, www.jacoblake.com.
Grand Canyon National Park: Fee. (928) 638-7888, www.nps.gov/grca.
Pipe Spring National Monument: Fee. (928) 643-7105, www.nps.gov/pisp.
Red Pueblo Museum: Fee. 1145 N. Main St., (928) 643-7777.
BLM Field Office Kanab, Utah: 745 US 89, (435) 644-1300, www.blm.gov/visit/kanab-visitor-center.
Kane Country Visitor Center: 78 S. 100 E., (800) 733-5263, www.visitsouthernutah.com.

Kaibab Plateau–North Rim National Scenic Byway

Overview This scenic road rambles across the broad back of the Kaibab Plateau through pristine forests and vast meadows to arrive at the North Rim of the Grand Canyon.

Route Numbers Arizona State Highway 67.

Mileage The scenic road is 30.3 miles (Milepost 580 to Milepost 610.3).

Special Notes The North Rim has a short season. All North Rim lodging and restaurants are open May 15 through October 15. The park remains open for day use until December 1 or until snow closes Arizona 67. Expect severe winter weather conditions. To access the road requires travel on Fredonia-Vermilion Cliffs Scenic Road.

Although they both overlook the earth's most glorious wound, the North Rim and South Rim of Grand Canyon have little else in common. They are separated by more than just the abyss.

Of the six million people that visit Grand Canyon National Park each year, only about 10 percent make the long winding drive to the North Rim, which rises 1,000 feet higher than its southern counterpart. Lack of crowds translates to a vastly different experience. North Rim visitors will encounter more elk, deer, and wild turkeys than tour groups. There are no helicopter rides, shuttle buses, and no bustling village.

Obviously, it's peaceful—but it's more than that. Atop the lonely Kaibab Plateau, the North Rim is defined not just by elevation but by isolation—a free-floating sanctuary cloistered and cocooned. This is an alpine outback of sun-dappled forests interrupted by luxuriant meadows drenched in wildflowers.

Even the prelude to the North Rim drive

A bison herd can often be found grazing in the lush meadows near the North Rim entrance of Grand Canyon National Park. Courtesy of Mike Koopsen, Sedona.

is dazzling as you travel the Fredonia–Vermilion Cliffs Scenic Road across the Arizona Strip. In the midst of this big empty land sits a speck of civilization, a hamlet known as Jacob Lake. The official drive begins here on Arizona 67. It's the only paved road leading to the North Rim some 44 miles to the south. But don't be in such a hurry to get started. First, have a cookie.

If there's anything better than a middle-of-nowhere fresh-baked cookie, I don't know what it could be. Jacob Lake Inn does a little bit of everything. They operate a motel with cabins, a gas station, general store, restaurant, and bakery. People remember them for their fat chewy cookies. Along with traditional favorites like oatmeal raisin, there's also a mad scientist/drunken

Travel Note On the east side of the highway, the Jacob Lake Lookout Tower rises above the trees. The hardworking men of the Civilian Conservation Corps erected the 80-foot steel tower in 1934. Visitors are welcome to climb up and enjoy the view.

Martha Stewart vibe emanating from the kitchen, producing some surprising cookie combinations like lemon-zucchini and chocolate parfait. I have a special weakness for the chocolate raspberry. A sackful makes a wonderful traveling companion.

Next to the inn is the Kaibab Plateau Visitor Center, a good place for maps, books, souvenirs, or just general information about the area and the national park.

Jacob Lake is named for Jacob Hamblin, a Mormon missionary and diplomat to several Native American tribes in the Southwest. It was Hamblin who negotiated safe passage from local Natives for explorer John Wesley Powell during his second expedition in 1871.

Despite the impressive pedigree of its name, this is a lake only by Arizona standards—a small pond that lets the local deer population wet their whistles. But it's a permanent water source and there aren't many of those atop this porous limestone plateau. The pond is located down a dirt road, a mile from the Kaibab Plateau Visitor Center in a field across from the historic Jacob Lake Ranger Station, built in 1910.

Back on 67, continue south through heavy timber that breaks up suddenly, scarred by the 2006 lightning-sparked Warm Fire. But amid the bare, broken ponderosa trunks are fields of aspen saplings several feet high. Aspens are always the first trees to grow back in open space cleared by fire.

The intact forest of conifers resumes after a few miles. Fingers of meadows begin to spread the trees apart and then finally sweep them back away from the roadway altogether. Big grassy parks are framed by forests of Engelmann spruce, blue spruce, Douglas fir, and aspen. A couple of small ponds dot the meadows, thumbprints of water that look like they need to be mowed around the edges.

Travel Note Carved by the Colorado River, the Grand Canyon stretches for 277 miles, entirely within the borders of Arizona. It is 18 miles at its widest and over a mile deep in places.

Point Imperial makes an exquisite perch to celebrate the rising sun. Courtesy of Mike Koopsen, Sedona.

About 25 miles south of Jacob Lake another dollop of civilization spreads across DeMotte Park, a large meadow ringed with trees. On the east side of 67, the North Rim Country Store is stocked with supplies, drinks, and snacks. Across the road, the Kaibab Lodge rents cabins. Inside the main building is a restaurant, bar, and gift shop.

Visitors enjoy panoramas from the porch of North Rim's Grand Canyon Lodge. Courtesy of Mike Koopsen, Sedona.

Nearby a US Forest Service campground makes for a cool summer getaway. The 38 sites are scattered among the trees at 8,750-feet elevation. There are no hookups but plenty of sweet views.

Approaching the national park, I spot a sign not often seen in Arizona. It warns to be on the lookout for bison in the road. Bison are not native to the Grand Canyon. This herd was brought to the Kaibab Plateau in 1906 in an effort to breed them with cattle. The experiment didn't pan out, and the animals were sold to the Arizona Game and Fish Department. House Rock Wildlife Area served as the designated bison range, but here's the thing: bison are going to go where bison wants to go. In 2000, the herd moseyed across the plateau and into the national park where they stay most of the time.

Entering the park, the road winds for a few more miles through heavy timber. It passes the turnoff for the road leading to Imperial Point and Cape Royal, passes a couple of trailheads and the campground, and ends at the parking area for historic Grand Canyon Lodge.

As cul-de-sacs go, this one is hard to beat. Step out of your car and walk past cabins scattered among the pine trees until suddenly you come upon the gash to end all gashes, the great cosmic bite mark, the Big Ditch. For many Grand Canyon connoisseurs, the North Rim is the only rim. I am not that way. I like to visit the canyon a lot, and the South Rim is open year-round and provides quick access. I wouldn't trade that for anything.

Yet I won't deny that a special kind of serenity blankets the North Rim. And it does provide you with a fresh perspective peering into the abyss. Angles are different.

A hiker climbs the North Kaibab Trail. Courtesy of Mike Koopsen, Sedona.

The formations feel closer and colors more vibrant. Without the crowds barnacled to your elbow, it's easy to forge a personal relationship with this crooked jack-o'-lantern grin of a gorge.

Start with a quick introductory hike (and this will likely be the most crowded spot you'll find on the North Rim) as you walk off the back porch of Grand Canyon Lodge and right onto Bright Angel Point Trail. This short (half-mile) but moderately steep paved path follows a narrow ridge poking into the maw. The dramatic viewpoints are accented by the sharp drop-offs—and you're never really sure whether it's the high elevation or the whiff of peril that causes your heart to pound. Welcome to the Grand Canyon.

More Scenic Driving

Cape Royal Road branches off from the North Rim Parkway, heading east. About 5 miles in, the paved road reaches a Y intersection. The left fork makes a 3-mile journey to Point Imperial with its regal vistas. At 8,803 feet this is the highest point on either rim. Continuing toward Cape Royal, the road stops at multiple canyon overlooks along the way, including Vista Encantada and Roosevelt Point. At the end of the road, the Cape Royal Trail makes an easy half-mile stroll along the rim with views of the Colorado River and the natural arch known as Angels Window. This is also a popular spot for sunrise and sunset viewing.

Hiking

UNCLE JIM TRAIL

Named for a former game warden, this 5-mile loop swings through a mixed conifer forest. It overlaps with the Ken Patrick Trail for the first mile before turning off. Uncle Jim Trail angles downhill, crossing a little drainage. The loop begins at the next intersection. Take either branch through quiet forest. Downed logs crisscross meadows, ferns blanket slopes, and clusters of lithe aspen saplings fill open spaces created by burn scars. The trail traces the head of Roaring Springs Canyon, and the trees often break apart—offering tantalizing views. Mule riders also use the trail, but for veteran canyon hikers, eau de donkey is a familiar perfume. Just watch where you step. Begin from the North Kaibab Trail parking lot.

CAPE FINAL TRAIL

Wander through open ponderosa pine forest across the Walhalla Plateau with almost no change in elevation. Leaving from Cape Royal Road, the trail brushes past a few choice canyon overlooks, but this is just the warm-up. The last section of the 2-mile path cuts through a woodland of oak and juniper ending atop a sprawling promontory with eye-popping views of rocky formations falling away from the rim. Tucked among the waves of terraced buttes, snippets of river are visible below, frothy with white water.

NORTH KAIBAB TRAIL

From the North Rim, only one maintained trail penetrates the depths of the canyon. The North Kaibab drops steeply through big timber. Groves of tall Douglas firs, Engelmann spruce, and ponderosa pines follow you downhill as you reach the Coconino Overlook at 0.7 miles. If you have the time and stamina, continue to Supai Tunnel, 1.7 miles from the rim. This 20-foot-long corridor is blasted from solid rock, and there are toilets and drinking water. It's a steep climb back out. Trailhead is on the park entrance road 1.5 miles north of Grand Canyon Lodge.

Information for all hiking trails: (928) 638-7888, www.nps.gov/grca.

Where to Eat and Stay

JACOB LAKE INN

Man does not live by cookies alone—although what a happier place this world would be if we did. Fortunately, the restaurant at Jacob Lake Inn serves up more substantial fare for breakfast, lunch, and dinner. Grab a table in the café or a seat at the old-time lunch counter. Plenty of traditional favorites to choose from, with some extras at dinner like spicy jalapenos meatloaf. (928) 643-7232, www.jacoblake.com.

GRAND CANYON LODGE

If you want to chow down in the elegant dining room perched on the rim, make reservations pronto. A restaurant with a wall of windows overlooking the Grand Canyon fills up quickly. The good news is the quality of food matches up with the quality of the views. The menu emphasizes contemporary and regional dishes like elk chili and fresh Utah trout. More casual fare can be found at the adjacent deli. The lodge offers a variety of surprisingly comfortable cabins just footsteps from the canyon; others are spread among the trees, with motel rooms within walking distance. (877) 386-4383, www.grandcanyonforever.com.

KAIBAB LODGE

Located just 5 miles from the entrance to the national park, Kaibab Lodge sits at the edge of a large meadow abutting a forest of aspens and evergreens. The rustic cabins come in a variety of sizes to accommodate different groups. There's no Wi-Fi or television, but you will likely have mule deer grazing out your front door. A dining room serves breakfast and dinner, and they'll even make a sack lunch if you want. The big stone fireplace in the lodge is almost always a welcome sight here at 8,770 feet. (928) 638-2389, www.kaibablodge.com.

When You Go

Jacob Lake Inn: (928) 643-7232, www.jacoblake.com.

Kaibab Plateau Visitor Center: (928) 643-7298.

North Rim Country Store: (928) 638-2383.

Grand Canyon National Park: Fee. (928) 638-7888, www.nps.gov/grca.

ROUTE 66

Historic Route 66 All-American Road (Ash Fork to Lupton)

Overview Although fragmented, the Route 66 segments that are still intact across Eastern Arizona capture the mystique of American travel throughout the twentieth century. This is one of two All-American Roads in the state—considered a destination unto itself—and is also a National Scenic Byway.

Route Numbers Historic State Route 66, Interstate 40, and a variety of local and state highways.

Mileage The National Scenic Byway covers 30.19 miles in varying segments. It is 213 miles from Lupton to Ash Fork.

Special Notes Traveling this route requires entering and exiting I-40 multiple times. This road connects to Historic Route 66 All-American Road (Topock to Ash Fork), Diné Tah "Among the People" Scenic Road, and San Francisco Peaks Scenic Road. It provides access to the Sedona–Oak Creek Scenic Road. The Navajo Reservation observes daylight saving time, although the rest of Arizona does not.

I think the Arizona Department of Transportation misses the mark with their official names of the two segments of Route 66. They are named west to east. That feels misleading. While many folks travel the old highway in that direction, it is not historically accurate.

For decades, the natural flow of movement along US 66 was from the east where most people lived to the sparsely populated but dramatic western lands. Depending on the decade, travelers came looking for

Petrified Forest National Park also protects the stark, colorful hills of the Painted Desert. Courtesy of Mike Koopsen, Sedona.

everything from the open road to the promised land. Since the call of the West still rings loud and true, that's how Route 66 should still be experienced—especially by those seeing it for the first time.

Route 66 was established on November 11, 1926. It opened with great fanfare connecting Chicago to Los Angeles, over 2,400 miles of road passing through eight states. In Arizona it flows in a pretty direct east-to-west line, following an already well-traveled corridor. In 1857, Lt. Edward Beale established a wagon road from Fort Smith, Arkansas, to Los Angeles along the thirty-fifth parallel. When the railroads came to the Arizona Territory in the 1870s and 1880s, tracks followed that same course.

In the 1930s, farmers from the Midwest poured onto Route 66 in search of a new life as they fled the devastating dust storms that consumed the land. This era led to the highway's most memorable nickname. In his 1939 novel *Grapes of Wrath*, John Steinbeck coined the term "mother road," and Mother Road it's been ever since.

During World War II, both equipment and troops flowed along Route 66. Military installations sprang up in the West, and war industry jobs drew even more migrating workers. But it was after the war that 66 truly blossomed. In 1946 Bobby Troup penned a little ditty encouraging Americans to get their kicks on Route 66, and that's just what they did. For most of the next two decades, the Mother Road blazed at night, a thin Milky Way of neon, stoplights, and headlights. Families vacationed, and people relocated or just moved across the country reveling in their newfound freedom and the absolute certainty that something wonderful waited in a town just down the road.

Travel Note Most of the Route 66 Arizona towns originated as railroad stops. Holbrook, Winslow, Seligman, and Kingman are all named for railroad officials or financiers.

The most famous corner on all of Route 66 can be found in Winslow, Arizona. Photo by the author.

Then interstates crashed the party. Certainly a nationwide network of high-speed roadways was necessary for continued prosperity. Yet when they became our primary mode of travel, something was lost as well.

Route 66 begins its journey across the Grand Canyon State at the small town of Lupton, which teeters on the Arizona–New Mexico border. A handful of colorful trading posts nestle at the base of soaring sandstone cliffs, among them a collection of shops that fall under the umbrella of the Chief Yellowhorse Trading Post.

Most of the eastern half of Route 66 is submerged beneath I-40, leaving orphaned segments at exits and towns. There are also frontage roads that connect a few of these exits. In some cases these are old 66 alignments, but not all. Various touristy trading posts are located at several of the little towns on the Navajo Nation such as Allentown, Houck, Sanders, and Chambers.

The scenery takes a dramatic turn as you pull into the Painted Desert. Stark but colorful badlands roll across the land like the waves of some psychedelic ocean. This haunting terrain is part of Petrified Forest National Park, the only national park crossed by Route 66. A 28-mile scenic drive cuts from the Painted Desert north of the interstate to the Petrified Forest south of it. Along the way are pullouts, overlooks, historic sites, and a few short trails (see Hiking).

This arid land was once a subtropical floodplain. During the Triassic Period, downed trees accumulated in river channels and were buried in sediment containing volcanic ash. The mixture of sediment, water, and ash saturated the trees, gradually turning the organic matter into quartz crystals. Other minerals caught up in the process added splashes of vivid color.

It was during this time, some 225 million years ago, that giant crocodile-like creatures and early dinosaurs roamed the landscape. You can see fossils and replicas of the animals and plants on display at the Rainbow Forest Museum at the southern end of the park.

Continuing west, Holbrook is the first Arizona Route 66 town with some size, offering multiple dining and lodging options, including the iconic Wigwam Motel. Stop by the historic Navajo County Courthouse, where you'll find the visitor center and museum. Old West buffs should grab a map for the downtown walking tour that includes Bucket of Blood Saloon and the Blevins House, site of a celebrated gunfight that was part of the Pleasant Valley War (see Desert to Tall Pines Scenic Road). Sheriff Commodore Perry Owens attempted to serve a warrant on Andy Blevins, which prompted the drawing of weapons. When the smoke cleared, three men were dead and another wounded. The sheriff walked away without a scratch.

While Winslow is the next big town, be sure to stop first at Jackrabbit Trading Post on the edge of Joseph City. Jackrabbit was made famous by an enigmatic advertising campaign of yellow billboards adorned with the profile of a black bunny and ever-changing mileages that were spread across the country. Besides a great selection of Route 66 gifts and memorabilia, the trading post is guarded by a giant fiberglass rabbit wearing a saddle. Mount up for a photo op, then go inside and support a local business.

Winslow was once so bustling the main drag (Route 66, of course) had to be divided into separate one-way streets through downtown. The community fell on hard times when I-40 siphoned off their flow of traffic but is finding its way back. No self-respecting Mother Roader misses a chance to stop in Winslow for two primary reasons: La Posada and a street corner.

La Posada Hotel was the last of the great Santa Fe Railway hotels, opened in 1930. It was considered architect Mary Colter's masterpiece. Closed for years and destined for a date with the wrecking ball, it was saved not by the government or big corporations but by individuals. That's very much the story of the rebirth of Route 66.

In the early 1970s, Jackson Browne wrote most of a song called "Take It Easy" but when he got stuck he gave it to his neighbor, Glenn Frey, who finished it in fine style. Frey sang it with the group he founded, The Eagles, and made it a hit. Of course there were a lot of hit songs from that era, and they live on only in faded memories and on classic rock radio stations. But this little ditty about running down the road resonated and endured. And because it contained the line, "Well, I'm standing on a corner in Winslow, Arizona . . ." our young dreams were given a home. We knew where the road led—it took us to Winslow and the promise of love: "It's a girl my lord in a flatbed Ford, slowing down to take a look at me." Winslow built a monument on a downtown corner a block from La Posada and it has become a beloved destination. It draws millions of visitors who come to do nothing but stand. On a corner. In Winslow, Arizona. It's an amazing spot at the intersection of Youth and Adventure. How kind of Jackson Browne and Glenn Frey to draw us a road map so we can return whenever we feel the urge.

Continuing west, Meteor Crater may just be a giant hole in the ground, but it's one of the most scientifically significant sights on 66. It's the best-preserved impact crater on earth and has been studied for decades. When NASA planned their first moon landing, they needed a place for the astronauts to train and they found it here on Route 66. How cool is that? The interactive museum includes exhibits and a short film. There are multiple viewpoints of the crater.

Watch for Two Guns, one of Route 66's eeriest ghost towns. A series of crumbling ruins are spread across the high plains, perched on the edge of Canyon Diablo. A historic Luten arch bridge still spans the canyon. Two Guns sits on private land, so respect all signs and gates.

Try not to sing snippets of the Route 66 song as you breeze through Winona, I dare you. You've left the prairie behind and are entering the pine forests surrounding Flagstaff. The outline of the San Francisco Peaks dominates the skyline. Three national monuments perch to the east and north of Flagstaff and tell a history much older than the Mother Road. You'll find remarkably preserved pueblos of the Sinagua culture dating back centuries at Walnut Canyon (located on one of the 66 alignments) and Wupatki, and the hulking volcano that erupted just a thousand years ago at Sunset Crater.

Follow Route 66 from East Flag to a buzzy downtown that lies north of the railroad tracks and the eclectic Southside District just across the rails, adjacent to the campus of Northern Arizona University. It's a great spot for walking around amid the shops, galleries, restaurants, and bars.

The distinctive 1927 Santa Fe depot houses the visitor center with answers for all your questions. They have brochures for several self-guided walking tours through the historic downtown including one that highlights the Mother Road, featuring the original alignment along Mike's Pike. You'll also find additional information on Flagstaff's lunar legacy. The mountain town was at the center of training for the Apollo astronauts in the 1960s and '70s. Every man who flew to or walked on the moon spent time preparing in the crater fields of Flagstaff, as well as exploring Grand Canyon and Meteor Crater.

Sitting 33 miles west of Flagstaff, Williams was the very last of the Route 66 towns. During the 1980s, a flurry of interstate building was underway, designed to replace the old road. Williams fought to preserve its Mother Road legacy, even filing lawsuits to prevent the completion of I-40. They finally lost the battle in court, and in 1984 Williams, Arizona, became the last Route 66 town bypassed by the freeway.

Lean years followed. The endless traffic that once flowed right through town now

Live music, the glow of neon, and cool mountain air makes Williams a perfect Route 66 destination on summer evenings. Photo by the author.

Travel Note In 2001, Flagstaff was named the world's first International Dark Sky City for its efforts in eliminating light pollution and preserving star-laden skies.

roared past on the super slab. But Williams clawed its way back. The turnaround began when Grand Canyon Railway resumed operations in 1989. Soon afterward restoration began on downtown buildings. In recent years, Bearizona Wildlife Drive-Thru Park opened, offering visitors a chance for an up-close encounter with a variety of animals, big and small.

I'm happy to report Williams feels vibrant again all summer long. Stores stay open late, and the sidewalks bustle with people. Music from street-side patios drifts up and down the boulevard, and everything is awash in the liquid velvet of neon. As traffic slow rumbles up and down old 66, it's easy to lose track of the decades.

It's another 18 miles to Ash Fork, where the western portion of the Route 66 journey begins.

Hiking

MARTHA'S BUTTE

You'll find a few short hiking trails in Petrified Forest National Park, plus Off the Beaten Path outings. These are cross-country treks, requiring navigational skills. The short journey to Martha's Butte is a good introduction to the backcountry experience. It's a 1-mile hike to a distinctive hill. Since the butte and road are always within sight, it's tough to get lost. Several boulders scattered around the base of the butte are adorned with petroglyphs. Starting point for the hike is near Dry Wash Bridge on the main park road. Fee. (928) 524-6228, www.nps.gov/pefo.

FATMANS LOOP #25

This popular Flagstaff hike snakes up the slope of Mt. Elden through pinewoods and a garden of boulders. There are a few short steep segments but nothing strenuous. Views of Elden, the surrounding landscape, and the town are really special on this 2-mile loop. Craggy rock formations serve as a reminder of Mt. Elden's volcanic past. At one spot the trail makes a reasonably tight squeeze between boulders earning its name. Fatmans Loop begins at the Elden Lookout Trailhead along US 89 in East Flag across from the mall. (928) 526-0866, www.fs.usda.gov/coconino.

BILL WILLIAMS MOUNTAIN TRAIL #21

Bill Williams was an itinerant preacher who set out to convert the American Indians but instead became enamored of their beliefs. He chucked his former life, lived among the Osages, and became a trapper, guide, translator, and all-around colorful mountain man. A forested trail makes its way up the mountain that bears his name overlooking the town that does likewise. The trail crosses Cataract Creek and winds its way up the slope, first through oak and pine and finishing amid fir and aspen. Long straight stretches are interrupted by carved switchbacks. The climb will definitely get your attention but is not as grueling as some mountain treks. It's 4 miles to the summit crowned with a bristling assortment of communication towers. (928) 635-5600, www.fs.usda.gov/kaibab.

Where to Eat and Stay

LA POSADA HOTEL, WINSLOW

The airy, romantic hacienda-style building has been painstakingly restored. Elegant rooms are named for the many celebrities who stayed here. Shady lawns and gardens surround the property that is flanked by the railroad in the back and Route 66 in the front. Even if you're not a guest at La Posada, stop and enjoy the architectural details and artwork on display. The Turquoise Room dishes up world-class cuisine, often while utilizing native and nearby ingredients. The locally harvested squash blossoms stuffed with sweet corn, Oaxaca cheese, and fried crispy in a beer batter are always a favorite in season. 303 E. Second St., (928) 289-4366, www.laposada.org.

ROUTE 66 DOG HAUS, FLAGSTAFF

Not many hot dog stands open early in the morning. But not many are as revered for their breakfast burritos as their franks as Route 66 Dog Haus. Customers can walk up to the window or order at the tunnel-like drive-thru in the middle of the big A-frame structure. Shaded picnic tables are available. An interesting bit of Route 66 history; this is actually the corner that Jackson Browne had in mind when he began writing "Take It Easy," but he decided ". . . standin' on a corner in Winslow, Arizona" sounded better than Flagstaff. 1302 E. Route 66, (928) 774-3211.

GLOBETROTTER LODGE, HOLBROOK

A once decrepit motor court located directly across the street from the Wigwam Motel was salvaged and then reinvented by an Austrian couple. Rooms at Globetrotter Lodge are spotless, homey, and full of personal touches like handmade furniture, bookshelves, and colorful tile sinks. The pool has also been restored. A filling continental breakfast is served in a sunny room off the lobby. 902 W. Hopi Dr., (928) 297-0158.

WIGWAM MOTEL, HOLBROOK

Reservations can be hard to snag during summer months because what kind of Route 66 traveler doesn't want to sleep in a giant teepee-shaped room? Opened in 1950 by Chester Lewis, the Wigwam Motel became an instant classic. Still operated by the Lewis family, the rooms have been upgraded but look very much like they always did. Vintage cars are parked on the property, and you know you're traveling Route 66 when you're snoozing in a wigwam. 811 W. Hopi Dr., (928) 524-3048, www.sleepinawigwam.com.

When You Go

Navajo Tourism Department: (928) 810-8501, www.discovernavajo.com.
Petrified Forest National Park: Fee. (928) 524-6228, www.nps.gov/pefo.
Holbrook Chamber of Commerce: 100 E. Arizona St., (928) 524-6558, www.holbrookazchamber.org.
Winslow Chamber of Commerce & Visitors Center: 523 W. Second St., (928) 289-2434, winslowarizona.org.
Meteor Crater: Fee. (800) 289-5898, www.meteorcrater.com.
Flagstaff Convention and Visitors Bureau: 1 E. Route 66, (928) 213-2951, www.flagstaffarizona.org.
Walnut Canyon National Monument: Fee. (928) 526-3367, www.nps.gov/waca.
Wupatki National Monument: Fee. (928) 679-2365, www.nps.gov/wupa.
Sunset Crater National Monument: Fee. (928) 526-0502, www.nps.gov/sucr.
Williams Visitor Center: 200 W. Railroad Ave., (928) 635-4061, www.experiencewilliams.com.
Grand Canyon Railway: Fee. (800) 843-8724, www.thetrain.com.
Bearizona Wildlife Drive-Thru Park: Fee. (928) 635-2289, www.bearizona.com.

The longest unbroken stretch of Route 66 still in existence crosses western Arizona. Photo by the author.

Historic Route 66 All-American Road (Topock to Ash Fork)

Overview This is the heart of the Route 66 experience. As it crosses the high plains of Northern Arizona, it visits the Birthplace of Historic Route 66 and travels through canyons, mountains, deserts, and small towns on the longest unbroken stretch of the Mother Road still in existence. This is one of two All-American Roads in the state—considered a destination unto itself—and is also a National Scenic Byway.

Route Numbers Historic State Route 66, Interstate 40.

Mileage The National Scenic Byway is 151.93 miles. It is 167 miles from Ash Fork to Topock.

Special Notes This road crosses the Hualapai Reservation. It connects to Historic Route 66 All-American Road (Ash Fork to Lupton) and provides access to Joshua Forest Scenic Road.

Ash Fork originated as a water stop on the railroad line. Later it had to contend with the loss of the Mother Road and devastating fires in the 1970s and '80s. But the "Flagstone Capital of the World" keeps chugging on. Don't miss the terrific museum that also serves as a visitor center. Housed in the old highway maintenance building, the Ash Fork Route 66 Museum is packed with memorabilia, artifacts, and dioramas. This is also a good place to grab a map for the Stone to Steel Dam Trail (see Hiking).

Juan Delgadillo built the Snow Cap in 1953 from scrap lumber, and it has been a Route 66 institution ever since. Photo by the author.

Just 4 miles west of Ash Fork, everything changes. At Crookton Road (Exit 139), say goodbye to the interstate for good. By making this choice, you are confirming that you're the type of traveler that values adventure over speed, experience over efficiency. Bravo.

This marks the beginning of the longest unbroken stretch of Route 66 still in existence, 158 miles to the California border. The long seductive ribbon of pavement stretches across a bewitching landscape. Sprawling country is draped by an uninterrupted sky and dotted by towns rooted in the past where classic cars, roadside attractions, and the soft knife of neon are still common sights. It's nice to know bygone days aren't gone at all. They just live along Route 66.

Almost immediately you're greeted by a poetic blast from the past: re-created Burma Shave signs spreading snippets of roadside rhyme. You'll see plenty more over the coming miles. Soon you're rolling into the heart of Seligman on wide lanes that once accommodated thousands of vehicles daily. Route 66 was created with two purposes in mind: to increase the flow of commerce from east to west and to be an economic engine to small towns. It certainly worked in Arizona where communities built their commercial district along this busy boulevard. That's how it earned another of its nicknames: "America's Main Street."

I first got interested in Route 66 because many years ago I stopped for a burger. I pulled off I-40 to eat in Seligman, a small town on the grasslands of Northern Arizona. A sign declared Seligman to be the Birthplace of Historic Route 66. But what caught my eye were four tour buses parked downtown.

It was Tuesday in the middle of nowhere, yet tour groups from France, Germany, and Japan were unloading. As I stood there, a group of motorcycle riders from Belgium roared up. Everyone streamed towards a small barbershop. Crowds that couldn't squeeze inside stood on the sidewalk snapping photos. I thought maybe Edward Scissorhands was working.

That was the day I met Angel Delgadillo, the small-town barber credited with leading the preservation movement that brought Route 66 back from the dead.

With the expansion of the interstate system, there seemed to be no more need for the old road. In 1985, just months after Williams became the last town bypassed, US 66 was officially decertified. All signs were taken down, and it was removed from maps. The highway immortalized by novel, song, film, and television, ceased to exist. America no longer had a Main Street.

Like many towns circumvented by the new interstate, Seligman struggled to survive. Traffic no longer streamed through downtown; it now hurtled past on I-40. Businesses shuttered, and residents fled. In 1987, Angel Delgadillo and his brother Juan organized a meeting of concerned residents. They formed the Historic Route 66 Association of Arizona, the first of its kind. They lobbied the state to designate Route 66 a historic highway and, lo and behold, they succeeded. That provided a blueprint for all other states to follow. That's how the Mother Road exists today, on a state-by-state basis as Historic Route 66.

Needless to say, Delgadillo—known as the "Guardian Angel of Route 66"—has become the most famous small-town haircutter in the world. He still holds court from his old barbershop, now the Route 66 Gift Shop and Visitor Center. He signs autographs, poses for photos, conducts interviews, and spins yarns to a rapt audience of travelers from around the globe.

All of Seligman has become the cradle for Route 66 nostalgia. This is where you'll find shops full of souvenirs, great eateries, motor courts, and tour groups speaking a variety of languages.

After crossing the wide Aubrey Valley pockmarked by prairie dog colonies (and reintroduced endangered black-foot ferrets), you'll reach Grand Canyon Caverns. I recommend a tour. You'll descend by elevator twenty-one stories underground into a massive cave and are guided through an immense series of chambers and tunnels past flowstone formations and walls twinkling with selenite crystals. For an unusual dining experience, grab lunch at the underground Caverns Grotto. Stouthearted guests can even spend the night in the Cave Room, a hotel suite 220 feet below the surface. Don't worry: this cave is dry, meaning it supports no life. No bugs or bats or other creatures. So if you do hear a noise in the middle of the night, it can only mean mole people are burrowing up from below attracted by the smell of your delicious skin.

The road curves to the southwest and enters Peach Springs. The small town serves as the administrative headquarters for the Hualapai Indian Nation. This is where you find Hualapai Lodge with a restaurant, a nearby convenience store, and a few historic buildings. You can also sign up for river tours, helicopter tours, and a visit to Grand Canyon Skywalk, which is a considerable distance away.

Just down the road, Keepers of the Wild in Valentine is a nonprofit rescue sanctuary for more than 150 abused, neglected, and abandoned exotic and indigenous animals. It's spread across the rocky hills at the edge of Crozier Canyon. This is one of my favorite places because they do such good work here giving animals that have had a bad break a second chance. It's always nice to take a tour and see gangs of tigers, lions, wolves, leopards, monkeys, and more lounging in roomy habitats and appearing playful and relaxed.

At the western end of Crozier Canyon, one of the true icons of Route 66 perches along a lonely stretch of highway. Hackberry General Store looks like a gust of wind might topple it into a heap of boards and rusty nails. But don't confuse dilapidated with abandoned. Unless you arrive at a weird random time, the dirt parking lot will likely be full. Tumbledown sheds, weathered signs, and vintage gas pumps surround the rickety main building. A fleet of rattletrap cars and trucks are scattered about the property. The impressive collection of Route 66 memorabilia belonged to a previous owner and has made Hackberry one of the most popular destinations on the Mother Road. Inside, wooden floors creak at every step. The walls and ceilings are upholstered with old posters, license plates, and patches. Artwork and Route 66 souvenirs spill from the shelves, but you can also purchase snacks and cold drinks. Expect to spend extra time here. There's a lot to take in, and you're not in any hurry. That's why you're driving the Mother Road.

A few miles farther west, Route 66 stretches through Kingman where you'll pass plenty of historic motels, eateries, and a restored train depot. Be sure to stop at the Kingman Powerhouse Visitor Center downtown. Built in 1907, the hulking concrete structure houses the Historic Route 66 Association of Arizona gift shop, the Route 66 Museum, and an Electric Car Museum. If you'd like to cool off, across the street is colorful Mr. D'z Route 66 Diner. Try a cold mug of their homemade root beer.

Travel Note Just west of Hackberry General Store, a striking 14-foot tall tiki-style head keeps an eye out for travelers. Known as Giganticus Headicus, the curious green artwork carries on a proud tradition of Route 66 roadside attractions. Pull over for a photo.

Outside town, the road flashes across sun-spanked desert before reaching the craggy foothills of the Black Mountains. Stop first at Cool Springs, a stunning recreation of a lonely gas station now functioning as a museum and gift shop in the shadow of Thimble Butte, a gnawed volcanic neck rising from the desert floor (see Hiking).

The next 8 miles into Oatman are a twisting mountainous climb. This steep grade and the desert heat punished early travelers but proves more thrilling than terrifying today. Lavish panoramas reveal themselves at every hairpin curve. The road weaves its way up through Sitgreaves Pass, past the Gold Road Mine and evidence of other small mining operations until you pull into town.

Oatman sags in a state of happy repose, casually picturesque and decidedly weird. A handful of historic buildings fronted by wooden sidewalks are strung along the highway. Stores are geared to Route 66 travelers selling gifts and souvenirs. There are also a couple of saloons and restaurants; the most notable is found in the Oatman Hotel dating back to 1902. Here the walls and ceiling are papered by dollar bills with names scrawled across them. The practice dates back to mining days when the men would post a dollar or two after payday so they could drink later when they were broke. I've got a couple of bucks stuck to the walls myself, which is a comfort at times. No matter what else happens in my life, I can always head for Oatman, pull down my dollars, and buy a beer. Or most of a beer. I better go back and post another dollar, just to keep ahead of inflation.

Gunfights break out in the street at

A signpost in Truxton offers helpful directions to Route 66 travelers. Photo by the author.

various times through the day, always a crowd-pleasing show. But Oatman is most famous for burros that loiter in the middle of town. Here's the really cool thing about that—the burros initiated the program! This wasn't put into motion by Oatman Chamber of Commerce, the Arizona Office of Tourism, or anyone else. These are descendants of animals released by miners. They live in the rough hills outside of town, foraging for food and dodging predators.

Then one day a burro worked up the gumption to visit town. Maybe someone felt sorry for him and dropped a piece of a sandwich. So he goes back to the herd and spreads the good news. The next day a couple of them go into town for more sandwiches and it just evolved.

Now it's a full-time job. Every morning the burros head into Oatman and stand around blocking traffic hoping to be fed. Water troughs are spread throughout the town. Stores sell bags of alfalfa cubes. The animals never bat an eye when gunfights break out in the street. At the end of the afternoon, just before shops close, all the burros mosey back into the hills. They repeat the scenario every day. Where else do critters organize a union and execute a business plan?

Keep in mind the Bureau of Land Management discourages the feeding of the burros or any wild animals—and I do too. Yet the Oatman burros are sort of the exception to that rule in my mind. They've carved out this whole way of life for themselves, and who am I to discourage that kind of initiative? So if you feel compelled to feed them, do not offer them carrots or anything other than the available alfalfa cubes. It's for their health and safety.

Over the years I've talked to many international travelers of Route 66, and almost invariably Oatman comes up over and over again as a favorite destination. The furry ambassadors create memories for folks all over the globe.

From Oatman, Route 66 continues through sparse desert spilling away from the mountains. It's 25 scenic miles to the California state line. Make your final stop at Topock 66 on the banks of the Colorado River, where you can take a swim, grab a bite, and raise a glass to the remarkable journey that is the Mother Road.

Hiking

STONE TO STEEL DAM TRAIL

Here's a weird engineering tidbit: the first large steel dam in the world was built in Ash Fork. In 1898, the Ashfork Bainbridge Steel Dam was constructed in remote Johnson Canyon to supply water for the railroad. Less than a mile upstream stands another dam, this one constructed from precision-cut stone blocks in 1911, also to supply water for the steam locomotives.

The two dams still back up lakes, now managed as recreational reservoirs. An easy path (0.35 miles) connects them. Exit I-40 at Welch Road east of Ash Fork. Travel north 0.3 miles. Veer left onto an old Route 66 segment and drive west 1.4 miles to Forest Road 6ED. Turn right and follow the good dirt road to the parking area. (928) 635-5600, www.fs.usda.gov/kaibab.

CAMP BEALE LOOP

The Camp Beale Loop in Kingman makes a meandering climb of 3.2 miles through lean grasslands punctuated by cactus and stands of yucca to a mesa top with expansive views of surrounding mountains and broad basins. During the 1870s, Camp Beale Spring occupied the flatland below, providing protection for Fort Mohave and Prescott Toll Road and serving as a supply station. Trailhead is off Fort Beale Drive. (866) 427-7866, www.gokingman.com.

MESA TRAIL

This path starts from the shoulder of Historic Route 66 directly across from Cool Springs. It slices through gaunt desert to the top of a stone-face promontory. Long, lanky switchbacks make for a moderate climb amid these hills populated with bighorn sheep and wild burros. Although it sits on private property, it is open to anyone. It was hand carved by the man who rebuilt Cool Springs. The trail hugs the flank of the hill, curling around toward the back and then zigzagging through a seam in the rocky crown. Hikers are welcome to explore the mesa top where you'll enjoy views of the Mother Road, Thimble Butte, and surrounding mountains. Just don't lose track of your way back down. It's just over a mile round trip.

It's rush hour in Oatman.
Photo by the author.

Where to Eat and Stay

SNOW CAP, SELIGMAN

Since 1953 the Snow Cap has been a beacon for hungry travelers, delivering not only great road food but also plenty of laughs. Juan Delgadillo, Angel's brother, built the little eatery from scrap lumber. He put his stamp of humor on everything and was known for his mischievous gags—like squirting patrons with mustard that was actually colored string and offering comically undersized and oversized servings—all done with a look of wide-eyed innocence and every now and then a flash of that contagious grin. Soon everyone wanted to stop and visit with the man known as the "Clown Prince of Route 66." Juan passed away in 2004, but his goofball traditions are in good hands as his family continues serving up the jokes (and memories) along with expertly prepared burgers, tacos, chicken sandwiches, and shakes. 301 Historic Route 66, (928) 422-3291.

FLOYD & CO. WOOD FIRED PIZZA, KINGMAN

This dapper little eatery has attracted attention for ambiance as well as food, a

Faded signs, vintage gas pumps, classic cars, and a mother lode of Mother Road memorabilia make Hackberry General Store an irresistible stop on Route 66. Photo by the author.

welcome addition to Kingman. They create artisan wood-fired pies with hand-pulled mozzarella and high-quality toppings perched on a soft, luscious crust that retains a crunch. They also offer dessert pizzas, like the scrumptious Black and Blue, blackberries and blueberries on a creamy honey base, topped with mint and powdered sugar. 418 E. Beale St., (928) 753-3626, www.floydandcompany.com.

EL TROVATORE MOTEL, KINGMAN

Treat yourself to a Route 66 experience with a night in one of Kingman's few motor courts built before World War II still standing. Their themed rooms pay homage to some of the notable icons that stayed here in the past like Clark Gable, Marilyn Monroe, and James Dean. These are vintage accommodations, not fancy but clean and fun. Perched on a hilltop, the towering neon sign will guide you home. 1440 E. Andy Devine Ave., (928) 753-6520, www.eltrovatoremotel.com.

When You Go

Ash Fork Route 66 Museum: 901 W. Route 66, (928) 637-0204.

Route 66 Gift Shop and Visitor Center: 22265 W. Route 66, (928) 422-3352, www.route66giftshop.com.

Grand Canyon Caverns: Fee. (928) 422-3223, www.gccaverns.com.

Hualapai Lodge: (928) 769-2636, www.grandcanyonwest.com.

Keepers of the Wild: Fee. (928) 769-1800, www.keepersofthewild.org.

Hackberry General Store: (928) 769-2605.

Kingman Visitor Center: 120 W. Andy Devine Ave., (866) 427-7866, www.gokingman.com.

Cool Springs: (928) 768-8366, www.route66coolspringsaz.com.

Oatman Chamber of Commerce: www.oatmangoldroad.org.

Topock 66: (928) 768-2325, www.topock66.com.

NAVAJO NATION

The distinctive spire of Spider Rock rises 800 feet from the floor of Canyon de Chelly. Courtesy of Mike Koopsen, Sedona.

Diné Tah "Among the People" Scenic Road

Overview Explore Navajo culture on a journey from the colorful buttes and mesas of the plateau country across forested mountains to one of the scenic wonders of Arizona. The road passes through the Navajo Nation capitol of Window Rock and ends at Canyon de Chelly National Monument.

Route Numbers Navajo Routes 12 and 64.

Mileage The scenic road is 100.3 miles (Milepost 0 to Milepost 100.3).

Special Notes The Navajo Reservation observes daylight saving time, although the rest of Arizona does not. This road provides access to Historic Route 66 All-American Road (Ash Fork to Lupton) and Tse'nikani "Flat Mesa Rock" Scenic Road.

One look at an Arizona map shows you that the entire northeastern portion of the state consists of the sprawling Navajo Nation, and the smaller Hopi Reservation. The Navajo Nation stretches for more than 27,000 square miles across Arizona, New Mexico, and Utah, and is the largest of all tribal lands in the United States. It is home to 200,000 of the Dinés (the Navajo people).

The Diné Tah Scenic Road winds through the heart of Navajoland, exploring a long and often tragic history and the scenic splendor of the landscape. It all starts at a very distinctive cultural crossroads. Lupton teeters on the far eastern edge of Arizona on the border with New Mexico. Interstate 40 flows through, and Lupton also serves as the terminus for Historic Route 66.

From Lupton take Indian Route 12 north along the Defiance Plateau. As soon as you leave behind the interstate and the tourist-aimed trading posts of Route 66,

Travel Note There are a few rules to follow while visiting the Navajo Nation. Respect the privacy and customs of the Navajo people. Do not approach private property uninvited. Do not photograph Navajos without their permission (a gratuity is expected). Alcoholic beverages are strictly prohibited. The use of firearms is illegal. Stay on designated roads. Rock climbing and off-trail hiking are prohibited.

everything seems to slow down. The land spreads out beneath a big expressive sky. Grasslands sweep up against a wall of sandstone running along the east side of the highway. Homes and farms and livestock are scattered among the expanse.

You'll reach Window Rock, the capitol of the Navajo Nation, as Indian Route 12 crosses Arizona 264. Window Rock is the site of government offices but also features an excellent museum and the Navajo Nation Zoo & Botanical Park filled with plants and animals important to Navajo culture and history. Most of the animals, residing in large natural habitats, were received as orphans or were too injured to return to the wild.

The Navajo Nation Museum maintains an extensive collection of photographs, documents, archaeological materials, art, and more. It's a good spot to learn more about the rich unique culture of the Navajo people.

A short detour leads to another interesting museum. The St. Michaels Historical Museum, located 3 miles west of Window Rock on 264, chronicles the lives of the Navajos in the early twentieth century. The St. Michaels Mission of Franciscan Friars was established in 1898 to teach the Navajo people. The original stone building contains exhibits and photographs from those early years and is open to the public on weekdays from Memorial Day to Labor Day. The mission and school still serve the Navajo community.

Back in Window Rock, the Ch'ihootso Indian Marketplace sits at the northwestern corner of Indian Route 12 and Arizona 264. Vendors display arts and crafts as well as traditional food items. If you're interested in trying local cuisine, this is a good place to start. Frybread, mutton stew, Navajo burgers, kneel-down bread, blue-corn cookies, and more are being served up.

Window Rock derives its name from the natural opening in the sandstone cliffs just north of town and is surrounded by a small park open to the public. In recent years they've built a veterans' memorial at the base of the arch to honor the many Navajos who served. Circular paths wind through the park and steel pillars list names of the veterans. A large sculpture of a kneeling marine radioing in a message commemorates the Navajo Code Talkers.

During World War II, a group of Navajo men used their native language to create a secret code for communications in the Pacific Theater that the Japanese were never able to crack. Their ability to quickly send and relay secure tactical messages proved decisive in several battles. Navajo Code Talkers saved countless lives and shortened the war.

While I had visited Window Rock in the past, the first time I saw the veterans' memorial proved especially significant. I had recently traveled to Ohio and visited with my uncle Raymond, my father's oldest brother who had just turned ninety. He had never talked much about World War II but, after a few questions on my part, finally revealed some details. He was in the Pacific Theater in late 1944. His unit was transporting mules near the Burma Road when they were hit by mortar fire, their first taste of combat. Raymond and two others were wounded. It took some daring flying to get them airlifted out of the mountainous region. None were expected to survive, and indeed the other two men didn't make it through the first night. After getting stitched up, Raymond was in the hospital for ten months.

The Navajo Code Talkers Veteran Memorial can be found in Window Rock. Photo by the author.

Exactly one week after I visited with my uncle, I stood in the Window Rock park seeing the Navajo Code Talker sculpture. It's a lovely tribute with the names of all the code talkers on the bricks surrounding the statue. While I was there, an elderly Navajo woman came to the memorial led by her grandchildren. They were looking for a specific name and after a long search they found it. I wandered away so as not to intrude on their private moment. The world can be so big, and the world can be so remarkably small. We were both there thinking about loved ones who served together in the same corner of the war all those decades ago.

Just a few miles north of Window Rock

is Fort Defiance. While the fort is long gone, replaced by a handful of businesses strung along the road, there is doubtless a painful stigma still attached. A military post was established in 1851 so the US Army could protect settlers moving into the area. In 1864, Fort Defiance became a concentration point where captive Navajos were forced on the "Long Walk." More than 8,000 Navajos were marched to Bosque Redondo and Fort Sumner, New Mexico, more than 300 miles across rugged terrain. They were held there for four years living in crude shelters and being ravaged by disease and starvation before being allowed to return to their homeland, the newly established reservation.

The road bends east leaving Fort Defiance, dipping into New Mexico, and then turning north again. It stays in the Land of Enchantment running parallel to the Arizona border for about 40 miles. And what a show it puts on as it rambles past an array of stunning cliffs, big waves of stone pushing north. Around every curve a different assortment of blocky buttes and mesas appear. Drop this range of cliffs into a national park, and tourists would be lining up to visit. Yet they seem quite natural simply framing a backdrop for a few farms and ranches in this quiet place.

The road begins to climb into the Chuska Mountains, leaving the rangeland behind for a forest of ponderosa pines. It reenters Arizona and soon skirts along the edge of Wheatfields Lake. Stocked each spring with rainbow trout, this is a popular spot for anglers and campers. A Navajo fishing license is required.

Not long after passing Wheatfields Lake, you'll reach the intersection with Indian Route 64 in the community of Tsaile. This is the location of Diné College, which is the oldest and largest tribally controlled college. The Ned A. Hatathli Cultural Center is designed to resemble an eight-sided hogan and contains a museum and gallery open to the public.

Travel Note The hogan is a traditional dome-shaped Navajo dwelling, with the door always facing east to greet the rising sun.

Turn left on 64, which curves to the southwest through open scrubland, giving no immediate sense of what lies beyond. This is the North Rim Drive of Canyon de Chelly National Monument.

The park contains a complex of canyons unlike anything else in the state. When we peer over a canyon edge, we expect to see a landscape rugged and wild. At Canyon de Chelly, a peaceful bucolic scene greets us. Sheer cliffs plunge hundreds of feet to lush bottomlands lined with corn crops, pastures, and cottonwoods. It's a staggering blend of high drama and pastoral beauty. The national monument shelters thousands of archeological sites and dozens of Navajo families that still live and farm there during summer months.

The North Rim Drive traces the edge of Canyon del Muerto with three viewpoints overlooking prominent cliff dwellings. I arrived late on a stormy summer evening and while I was eager to get to my motel in Chinle before night fell, I had to stop for a peek into the canyon even in the dim gauzy light. The western sky was seething with dark foreboding clouds, so I wasn't expecting much of a sunset. Then, as often happens during monsoon season, a sliver of open sky appeared atop the horizon. It was just wide enough for the setting sun to leak through, and using the clouds as reflectors, spray the land in a brief but intense shower of color. I was at the Antelope House Overlook and walked out onto the long slickrock ledge where potholes of rainwater had collected during the day. Sitting beside one of these small lizard lakes, I watched as the

Visitors can take the trail to White House Ruins without a Navajo guide. Courtesy of Mike Koopsen, Sedona.

water's surface turned into a flaming gold mirror. I stayed on that high ledge breathing cool rain-kissed air, embraced by soft shadows and an aching stillness. It was dark by the time I got to Chinle, but I no longer minded.

More Scenic Driving

Canyon de Chelly National Monument looks like a sideways V, with the narrow end pointed at Chinle, the town sitting just beyond the park boundary. The visitor center is also located at the narrow end where the canyons join with a nearby campground and picnic area. Canyon del Muerto forms the northern branch and Canyon de Chelly makes up the lower prong. Take the South Rim Drive (19 miles) to explore seven overlooks of Canyon de Chelly, each more spectacular than the last, culminating at the vista for Spider Rock, a slender pinnacle of rock rising 800 feet from the canyon floor. At White House Overlook, visitors can hike into the canyon along a breathtaking trail for an up-close look at a multi-tiered pueblo (see Hiking). Tours are available by jeep, horseback, and hiking. A group of registered tour operators are located near the visitor center on the South Rim Drive. Tours can also be booked at Thunderbird Lodge.

Hiking

WHITE HOUSE RUINS TRAIL

This trail is the only way to access the inner canyon without a Navajo guide. Despite switchbacking down a sheer rock face, the route never feels especially steep. It passes through a short tunnel at the top and another near the bottom. A few strategically placed benches provide welcome relief on the climb out. Upon reaching the canyon floor, a wooden bridge helps you cross the dry wash lined by cottonwoods. The trail ends at the base of the cliff sheltering the terraced ruin in a shallow alcove. The village once contained eighty rooms, and the building began about a thousand years ago. It's a round trip of 2.5 miles. (928) 674-5500, www.nps.gov/cach.

Where to Eat and Stay

NAVAJOLAND INN, ST. MICHAELS

Located 3 miles west of Window Rock near the historic St. Michaels Mission, this modern hotel offers comfortable if basic accommodations done in Southwestern style. The property includes an indoor pool and exercise room. 392 W. Arizona 264, (928) 871-5690, www.navajolandinn.com.

QUALITY INN NAVAJO NATION CAPITAL, WINDOW ROCK

Guests will enjoy clean, comfortable rooms, although nothing luxurious. A great base camp to explore the community since the hotel is within walking distance to the Navajo Nation Museum and Navajo Nation Zoological & Botanical Park. The Diné Restaurant is on premises and provides a complimentary breakfast for guests. The menu includes most items you expect to find at a hotel restaurant along with traditional Navajo dishes. 48 W. Arizona 264, (928) 871-4108.

THUNDERBIRD LODGE, CHINLE

This historic property sits at the mouth of Canyon de Chelly inside the national monument. Originally built as a trading post in 1896, the stone-and-adobe units maintain the rustic character of the original building. The cafeteria serves a selection of soups, salads, sandwiches, steaks, and a few Navajo dishes. The trading post still carries a selection of jewelry, rugs, pottery, and other works created by local artisans. You can also book tours of the canyon right from the lodge. (928) 674-5842, www.thunderbirdlodge.com.

When You Go

Navajo Tourism Department: (928) 810-8501, www.discovernavajo.com.
St. Michaels Historical Museum: (928) 871-4171.
Navajo Nation Museum: Arizona 264 and Loop Rd., (928) 871-7941.
Navajo Nation Zoo & Botanical Park: (928) 871-6574, www.navajozoo.org.
Wheatfields Lake: Navajo Nation Fish and Wildlife, (928) 871-6450, www.nndfw.org.
Ned A. Hatathli Cultural Center: (928) 724-6982.
Canyon de Chelly National Monument: (928) 674-5500, www.nps.gov/cach.

Pictographs adorn the walls of Canyon del Muerto. Courtesy of Mike Koopsen, Sedona.

Sandstone mesas, vertical cliffs, and towering monoliths are all defining features of the Navajo Nation in Arizona. Photo by the author.

Tse'nikani "Flat Mesa Rock" Scenic Road

Overview This road cuts through the exquisitely carved landscape of the Navajo Nation, past sandstone mesas, buttes, and towers in vivid hues of red and orange.

Route Numbers US 191.

Mileage The scenic road is 43.4 miles (Milepost 467 to Milepost 510.4).

Special Notes The Navajo Reservation observes daylight saving time, although the rest of Arizona does not. This road provides access to Diné Tah "Among the People" Scenic Road.

This is a road trip for the sake of a road trip. You'll find no amenities or tourist comforts along the 43 miles it covers. Far from the beaten path, the road delivers nothing but an authentic look at life on the Navajo Nation and some delicious scenery along the way.

Travelers looking for a leisurely journey will enjoy sandstone monoliths reminiscent of Monument Valley and colorful badlands that will call to mind the Painted Desert—both interspersed with sun-kissed rangeland beneath an azure sky.

The official scenic road begins in the small community of Many Farms, 16 miles north of Chinle and Canyon de Chelly National Monument. You'll find a couple of gas stations here, but not much else. Continue driving north on US 191, and you'll soon cross a wide arroyo, which just happened to be flowing with muddy water the last time I drove this route. I came in behind a summer storm and got to witness the normally arid landscape reveling in abundance. That's a bonus on any Arizona road trip.

Soon you're climbing into rumpled clay hills seamed with color. Clustered bare mounds line both sides of the road. The starkness of the terrain conflicts with the richness of the colors. It feels like I made a wrong turn and ended up on the surface of Mars.

A striking sandstone formation rises beyond the cluster of badlands. While snapping photos, I scrambled to the top of one of the highest of the clay hills for a better perspective. When I was ready to descend, my route suddenly seemed steep and perilous. I took one cautious downward step and realized that was it. There was no traction to hold me. My momentum had shifted and there was no stopping it. I was going to the bottom no matter what, whether upright or rolling head over heels.

While my first step may have been cautious, my second was a panicked stab and by the third was a full-throttle run. At this point I was just gravity's girlfriend. I went hurtling down the rain-slick clay, dodging holes and rocks, and when I finally hit a horizontal surface I must have sprinted a football field across the playa before I could stop. It is, I suppose, one of the allures of traveling. When we stumble on an adventure, big or small, planned or unplanned, enjoy the ride and try not to break your neck.

The badlands begin to thin and then break apart against long plains. But this is no run-away-to-the-horizon prairie. Everywhere red and orange sandstone mesas wall in the land. Some formations are dense and blocky, while others send up columns and spires with patches of blue sky peeking through the cracks, windows and arches carved by the ages. If erosion is not just a force of nature but an artist, the Navajo Nation is where it goes to perfect its craft.

Although expansive, the land is far from empty. Hogans, homes, pole corrals, pickup trucks, and even the occasional horseback rider can be seen scattered among the fields. Dirt roads wind through the sage and grass pointed toward distant ranches.

After about 10 miles, a stop sign marks the tiny settlement of Round Rock. The road that had been trending east now bends to the northwest. The scenery doesn't change; it only grows more enchanting. A long sliver of highway slices through a landscape hemmed in by exquisitely carved cliffs. This may not be a road for tourists, but travelers will love it.

Most of the time Lukachukai Creek is filled with nothing but sand and lizard tracks, but it was also running on my summer visit, prompting a stop. I can think of few sweeter sounds than the music of water flowing where water seldom flows. This landscape is veined by shallow arroyos that are perpetually dry. Then the rains come or the snows melt, and a phantom stream suddenly springs to life. This ethereal thing may exist only a matter of minutes or hours, sometimes longer. It is a blessing for however long its song lasts.

As you approach the community of Rock Point, more big stone towers seem to gather closer to the road. On the east side of the highway, look for the distinctive profile of Whale Rock. Two rocks form the outline of a partially submerged whale with head and tail rising from the water. Nothing seems too surprising in this dreamscape world.

You'll breeze through Rock Point pretty quickly, but there's a gas station and convenience store if you want to linger for a bit. Twin red monoliths create an interesting

Flat Mesa Rock Scenic Road offers no tourist amenities, just lots of sandstone scenery. Photo by the author.

skyline. When you continue north out of town, you'll pass through a wide tunnel of natural stone as rock walls seem to wrap around the pavement. A few miles later the road ends amid sandy plains at the junction of US 160.

Turn left on US 160, and it's 41 miles to Kayenta, where you'll find food, lodging, and the start of the Kayenta–Monument Valley Scenic Road. If you still have some time to explore, turn right and head for a unique intersection.

It's about 33 miles to Four Corners Monument. This is the only place in the country where four states come together, and if you ever made a family trip out west, chances are this was one of the stops. Visitors travel from all over just so they can engage in Twister-like contortions to simultaneously occupy Utah, Colorado, New Mexico, and Arizona—and, of course, to document the

Travel Note Navajo tacos are served open-faced using frybread as a base and topped with a landslide of beans or beef, lettuce, tomatoes, cheese, and more. Frybread, a golden wheel of dough puffy in the middle and crispy on the skin, originated during the Navajos' "Long Walk." To prevent mass starvation, the government issued a few meager rations of flour, sugar, salt, and lard. From such simplicity, frybread was created.

moment in a blaze of selfies. Local Navajo and Ute artisans are on hand selling crafts and food. One of the best Navajo tacos I ever ate was from a food truck at Four Corners, purchased I think in New Mexico and gobbled down at a picnic table in Utah.

The drive to Four Corners is lovely as well. Almost immediately after turning east onto US 160, you'll pass the Mexican Water Trading Post where you can also stop for a meal. It's 28 miles to Teec Nos Pos, which may be the most musical name of any Arizona community. Say it a few times when you're in a grouchy mood and see if it doesn't prompt a smile. Teec Nos Pos, Teec Nos Pos. It means "trees all around" in Navajo and is as pretty as the name implies.

Teec Nos Pos Trading Post, almost a poem unto itself, sits on the high plains, amid soft hills near a winding stream. This is one of the few traditional trading posts remaining, providing a variety of services to the local residents. This is where they come to get gas, groceries, hardware, hay, livestock feed, propane, and just about everything else. This is where they bring their arts and crafts to sell to the trader. Rug weavers from this area are known for a distinctive style using brown, black, and white yarn. If you're interested, ask to see the rug room.

From Teec Nos Pos, continue 5 miles to Four Corners.

Hiking

There are no designated hiking trails along this route. While the many rock formations can be very enticing, please note all areas on the Navajo Nation are closed to non-Navajos unless you have a valid camping, hiking, or backcountry permit issued by the Navajo Parks and Recreation Department. For information on permits, contact Navajo Parks and Recreation at (928) 871-6647, www.navajonationparks.org.

Public hiking trails are open in Monument Valley Navajo Tribal Park (see Kayenta–Monument Valley Scenic Road) and Canyon de Chelly National Monument (see Diné Tah "Among the People" Scenic Road). Other hikes can be taken in the company of a Navajo guide.

Where to Eat and Sleep

BEST WESTERN CANYON DE CHELLY INN, CHINLE

Located just minutes from Canyon de Chelly, the Best Western offers the most modern rooms in the area with all the conveniences you expect to find at a chain hotel. It includes an indoor pool. The Junction is the on-premises restaurant, and they serve homemade stews, Mexican and American items, some Navajo favorites, and, surprisingly, a couple of oriental dishes. 100 Main St., (928) 674-5875.

HOLIDAY INN CANYON DE CHELLY, CHINLE

Besides the comfortably appointed rooms, guests will enjoy an outdoor pool and shady courtyard at this Holiday Inn. The gift shop carries the work of local artisans. Garcia's Restaurant features a casual Southwestern atmosphere serving regional dishes. Besides the hotel eateries, the rest of the dining options in Chinle consists of fast food.

BIA Route 7—Garcia Trading Post, (928) 674-5000.

When You Go

Teec Nos Pos Trading Post: (928) 656-3224.

Four Corners Monument: Fee. (928) 206-2540, www.navajonationparks.org.

The iconic Mittens catch the light of a setting sun in Monument Valley. Courtesy of Mike Koopsen, Sedona.

Kayenta–Monument Valley Scenic Road

Overview Travel to one of the most famous and recognizable landscapes in the West defined by tall monoliths that split the sky in long vertical thrusts.

Route Numbers US Highway 163.

Mileage The scenic road is 27.71 miles (Milepost 389 to Milepost 416.71).

Special Notes The Navajo Reservation observes daylight saving time, although the rest of Arizona does not.

Close your eyes and picture the West—the Wild West, the Old West, the Hollywood West, or the Real West—it doesn't matter. Chances are the images in your head are of soaring spires, sculpted columns, and broad mesas—because if you're like me, you're seeing Monument Valley.

Straddling the Arizona-Utah border, Monument Valley is the centerpiece landscape of the Navajo Nation. Like Grand Canyon, Sedona's red rocks, and the towering saguaro cactus of the Sonoran Desert, this is a defining skyline of the state. Yet because of its isolated location, it receives only a fraction of the visitors as those other destinations.

The scenic road starts from the community of Kayenta sitting at the junction of US 160 and US 163. While definitely a small town, Kayenta serves as the central hub for this part of the reservation and includes all amenities such as lodging, food, and gas.

Before starting the journey, pay a visit to the local Burger King where you'll find more than fast food. The restaurant is the home of the Navajo Code Talkers Exhibit. Artifacts, photographs, and clippings are on display. Outside on the property is the

Navajo Shadehouse Museum. Take a self-guided tour of traditional Navajo structures while the small museum contains a treasure trove of jewelry, clothing, tools, war memorabilia, and cultural information.

Drive north on 163 where you'll quickly cross a deep defile carved by Laguna Creek. After climbing a ridge and rambling across sagebrush flats, a couple of notable formations pop up. That's Owl Rock on the west side of the highway. On the east side, the sharp steep crag of Agathla Peak rises above the valley floor. Also known as El Capitan, the eroded volcanic neck makes a distinctive landmark. It won't be the last one of those you see on this drive.

Continue across the wide prairie flanked by sandstone buttes and mesas. Hogans are scattered amid the sandy scrub, and horses and sheep graze nearby. I imagine it looks very much like it has for some centuries. After a few miles, the spires and buttes rising in the distance begin to look increasingly familiar. These are the rough bones of Monument Valley.

It's not really a valley in the traditional sense but an upwarp of sedimentary rock caused by volcanic pressure below the earth's surface. A plateau of layered sandstone and limestone once rose 3 miles above sea level. Millions of years of water and wind erosion have whittled the rocky remains into the graceful masterpiece we recognize today. A few million more years, and there won't be anything left standing in the valley. One more reason to plan your trip soon.

You'll enter Utah for a fleeting moment. When you turn on the road for the Monument Valley Navajo Tribal Park, you'll cross back into Arizona.

At the end of the 4-mile paved road,

From Hunts Mesa, panoramas extend across Monument Valley. Courtesy of Mike Koopsen, Sedona.

you'll find the visitor center and museum along with the Navajo-owned View Hotel, restaurant, trading post, and campground. Vistas from the overlook are spectacular and are worth the journey alone. If the word "panorama" didn't exist, we would have to invent it for Monument Valley. Once you're able to pull yourself away from the devastating overlooks, the visitor center contains a museum with exhibits on the cultural history of the tribe and the Navajo Code Talkers.

I can think of no place where the earth maintains such an intimate relationship with the sky as it does in Monument Valley. You know where one ends and the other begins, except then you don't. The sky floats to the ground here, slipping in between the towers, buttes, and mesas, keeping everything separate and distinct. The spaces between these shy formations become as haunting and memorable as the rocks themselves.

Monument Valley was set aside as the first tribal park. It shelters over 91,000 acres and is still home to dozens of Navajo families. The only public access to the interior of the park is a 17-mile dirt road (13 miles are one way) that loops through its stony heart. From the parking lot, the road slopes down to the valley floor passing the Mittens and Merrick Butte. This feels like the edge of the world, where every stone has one surface firmly on the ground and spears the clouds with the other end.

The road continues past such distinctive features as Three Sisters, John Ford Point, Rain God Mesa, North Window, and Totem Pole, all separated by a quiet expanse. It is a deliberate land where the silence is musical and there is a power to the sparseness. Loneliness has no negative connotations here.

High-clearance vehicles are recommended, but carefully driven passenger cars can generally manage the road. If you prefer to let someone else handle the wheel, take a jeep tour with a Navajo guide. You can sign up at a small booth in the visitor center parking lot with any one of several companies. Goulding's Lodge, sitting just outside the tribal park, also offers regularly scheduled tours. Besides the primitive road, some tours will explore distant corners of the terrain like Mystery Valley and Hunt's Mesa. Horseback and hiking tours are also available.

I often get asked to name my favorite Arizona hiking trail, which is an impossible task. I usually rattle off several to reflect the staggering diversity of the state. But if I had to pick just one, it would likely be the Wildcat Trail, a 3.2-mile loop that weaves among the iconic formations of Monument Valley (see Hiking). It has the power to transport me like no other trail. At one time, Wildcat was the only trail that could be taken in the park without a Navajo guide, but two more have been added to the roster, making Monument Valley an even more beloved destination for passionate bipeds like me.

No trip to Monument Valley is complete without a visit to nearby Goulding's Lodge, located on the west side of US 163 adjacent to the turnoff for the tribal park. Harry Goulding moved to Monument Valley in the early 1920s with his young wife Leone (who he affectionately nicknamed "Mike" because he had trouble spelling "Leone"). The couple built a trading post and eventually gained the trust of the Navajo people.

During the Great Depression, money and jobs were almost nonexistent on the reservation. Harry had the idea to attract Hollywood interest in Monument Valley as a movie location. Using their last $60, he and Mike traveled to the coast toting photos of the landscape. Harry finally wrangled a meeting with director John Ford. Ford must have liked what he saw because he came and shot the film *Stagecoach*.

John Ford Point is a popular vista on the 17-mile dirt road through Monument Valley Navajo Tribal Park. Courtesy of Mike Koopsen, Sedona.

Released in 1939, the epic tale transcended the Western genre and turned John Wayne into a breakout star.

Ford and Wayne would return over the years to make several more movies, providing jobs and capital for the tribe and putting Monument Valley on display to the world. The Gouldings built accommodations to house the film crews and that eventually grew into the lodge. Today, Goulding's has evolved into a sprawling complex that includes a grocery store, gas station, restaurant, gift shop, and a campground in a red rock canyon. The original store has been converted into a terrific museum. There's even a theater that shows John Wayne movies nightly.

Even though the official scenic drive ends at the tribal park, continue north on US 163 into Utah for more spectacular vistas. Just a few miles across the border is one of the best-known viewpoints of Monument Valley, near Utah Milepost 13. Gazing back toward Arizona, a long straight stretch of road with a slight hook at the end drops down from a hill toward a line of carved formations. It's a spot made famous, not by any cinematic gunfighter or cavalryman but by a bearded man-child. This is where Forrest Gump abruptly ended his cross-country run, much to the surprise of his gaggle of followers.

There are pullouts on either side of the road, but be alert for shutterbugs standing in the middle of the highway snapping away while someone re-enacts the Tom Hanks part. If you keep driving north, you'll cross the San Juan River and reach the town of Mexican Hat, Utah, 20 miles north of the Arizona border. Besides the signature rock formation that prompted the town name, you'll find a couple of small motels, restaurants, a saloon, and gas station.

Not surprisingly, the drive back to Arizona is stunning.

Hiking

WILDCAT TRAIL

The 3.2-mile loop throws a lasso around the West Mitten and provides spectacular views of East Mitten and Merrick Butte. It descends from the parking lot of the View Hotel to the valley floor. From there it is mostly level ground as the path circles through the sand and sagebrush for an up-close view of the massive formations. It's sun, sky, and stone in perfect balance. An aching stillness envelops the landscape. Don't be surprised if it is so quiet you can hear the sound of your beating heart.

MESA RIM TRAIL

Starting from the south side of the View Hotel along with the Lee Cly Trail, Mesa Rim branches off turning uphill. It makes a short (0.7 miles one way) but steep climb up the shoulder of the mesa above the hotel. The elevated perch offers a good vantage point for far-ranging vistas. But be alert. It's hard to tell exactly where the official trail ends. Some social pathways keep going up, and the footing becomes less stable the higher you go.

THE LEE CLY TRAIL

This pathway was dedicated in the summer of 2016 and makes a 2.1-mile loop across sandy hills with excellent views of Mitchell Butte, Mitchell Mesa, and Grey Whiskers Butte. Starting from the same spot as Mesa Rim, the trail stays mostly level but the deep sand gives you a bit of a workout. Lee Cly was born in Monument Valley and went on to become the longest serving ranger in the tribal park's history.

Information for all hiking trails: (435) 727-5870 www.navajonationparks.org.

Where to Eat and Stay

VIEW HOTEL

This is the only lodging within the tribal park. The View is designed to exist in harmony with the magnificent surroundings. It features a low contour conforming to the mesa it sits atop so as not to disrupt the scenery. The exterior's reddish hue blends with the rock. Rooms face east, each with a sheltered balcony framing a personal panorama of iconic formations. The View also features private cabins in Western décor overlooking the valley floor. A campground offers RV and tent sites. The restaurant overlooks the Mittens and serves traditional Navajo dishes as well as American items. Try the green chili stew. (435) 727-5555, www.monumentvalleyview.com.

GOULDING'S LODGE

Historic Goulding's Lodge sits at the base of Rock Door Mesa, adjacent to the tribal park. Southwestern-style rooms are clean and comfortable and come with private balconies. There are also sixty-eight hillside suites, which are standalone units with a separate bedroom, living room, kitchen, and porch. There are two heated indoor pools, one at the lodge and another at the campground. A variety of tours are available. The dining room is open for breakfast, lunch, and dinner and includes everything from thick steaks to a sampler of Navajo tacos. (435) 727-3231, www.gouldings.com.

When You Go

Monument Valley Navajo Tribal Park: Fee. (435) 727-5870, www.navajonationparks.org.

Naat'tsis'aan "Navajo Mountain" Scenic Road

Overview Dipping in and out of shallow canyons, and curving along the broad flank of White Mesa, this road cuts across colorful plateau country of the Navajo Nation to land on the banks of Lake Powell. Along the way, travelers will enjoy exotic formations and the 10,388-foot bulk of Navajo Mountain creasing the skyline.

Route Numbers Arizona State Highway 98.

Mileage The scenic road is 58 miles (Milepost 302 to Milepost 360).

Special Notes The Navajo Reservation observes daylight saving time, although the rest of Arizona does not. The road provides access to Fredonia–Vermilion Cliffs Scenic Road.

This highway starts from a lonely crossroads but ends with a dramatic flourish. Just don't be too eager to reach the finale because there is a lot to see along the way. The junction for Arizona 98 lies 32 miles southwest of Kayenta and 40 miles northeast of Tuba City. It rambles through wild lonely country for 58 miles until it lands on the rocky shores of Lake Powell.

In fact, before even starting out, take a detour. About a dozen miles northeast of 98, toward Kayenta, is the turnoff for Navajo National Monument. Look for Arizona 564 heading north off US 160. This has to be one of the shortest state highways in existence, traveling only 9 miles to the entrance of the monument.

Navajo National Monument protects remarkably preserved Ancestral Puebloan dwellings dating back centuries. The easiest to see is Betatakin. Built in a cavernous alcove in the canyon wall, Betatakin was occupied in the late 1200s. The ruins are visible from an overlook a half-mile from the visitor center, but for an up-close experience take a ranger-led tour conducted from spring through Labor Day. These strenuous 5-mile round-trip hikes are not recommended for anyone with health issues. Tours are limited to twenty-five on a first-come, first-serve basis. There are also

The Betatakin Pueblo is one of three ancient villages protected by Navajo National Monument. Courtesy of Mike Koopsen, Sedona.

Navajo Mountain rises above Lake Powell. Courtesy of Mike Koopsen, Sedona.

three short rim-top trails to be enjoyed anytime (see Hiking).

Advance reservations are required to see Keet Seel, the largest ancient cliff dwelling in Arizona. Only twenty people are allowed to visit per day. Sheltered by a massive rock overhang, Keet Seel is considered to be the most intact large site in the Southwest, looking very much like inhabitants left it seven hundred years ago. Granaries, pottery, petroglyphs, timbers, and corncobs give archeologists a glimpse at the distant past. The hike is a 17-mile round trip including a 1,000-foot climb down a cliff face and multiple stream crossings along the canyon floor. It can be done as a long day hike, or you can camp near the ruins. In the park, two campgrounds are also available on a first-come basis.

Travel Note The Shonto Rock the Canyon Arts & Music Festival is a swinging event held in early June each year.

When you're ready to tackle the scenic road, Arizona 98 will head north off of US 160 and then track northwest. It rambles through some wide-open spaces and across textured hills seamed with ledges of pink sandstone. Scattered groves of junipers and pinion pines are sprinkled across the terrain and provide some skinny shade for grazing sheep and horses. The road takes its name from Navajo Mountain, a peak that is sacred to several tribes including the Navajos, Hopis and Paiutes.

At 6 miles, it's time for another detour. But it's the last one, I promise. Look for the turnoff to Historic Shonto Trading Post, which dates back to 1914. It's 5 miles to Shonto, tucked in a high-walled canyon ringed by big cottonwood trees. I think it's one of the most scenic and out-of-the-way settings for a trading post on the reservation, and I always make a point to stop for a cold drink and a snack just to enjoy the picturesque surroundings. Not that they need my little dab of business. It always seems to be a bustling place, selling gas, groceries, propane, yarn, cleaning supplies, hardware, hay, and just about anything else you can think of. Shonto still operates out of the original building, a long, low stone structure. They also sell an assortment of rugs,

There's no mistaking the swooping curve of Horseshoe Bend along the Colorado River. Courtesy of Mike Koopsen, Sedona.

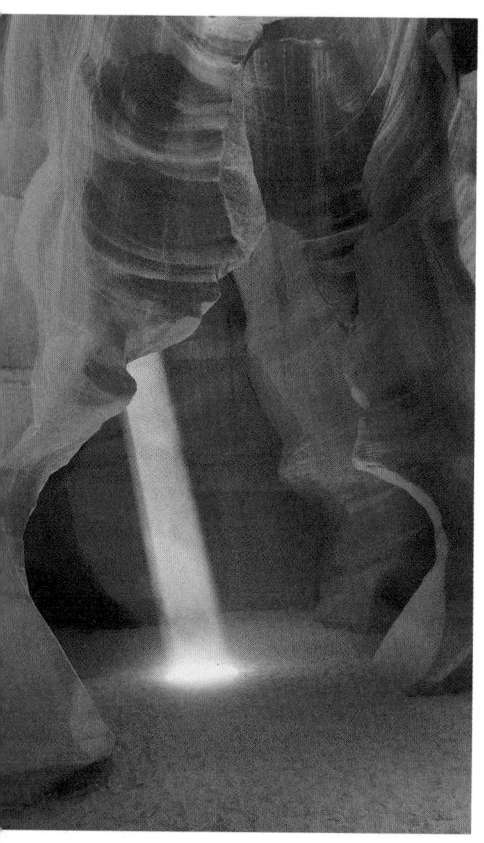

A spear of sunlight illuminates the swirling contoured walls of Antelope Canyon. Courtesy of Mike Koopsen, Sedona.

jewelry, pottery, paintings, and other work by local artisans.

Return to the scenic drive and continue across a landscape of prairie fractured by benches and ledges of sandstone with swirling strata. The rock formations may not be as distinctly dramatic along this stretch of road, but the way they are interwoven into the terrain make them just as spectacular.

The road climbs into a heavier concentration of pines, finally topping out at 6,687-feet elevation. A scenic pullout provides views of looming Navajo Mountain in the distance. Vendors often have tables set up here selling jewelry and other items. One of the artists tells me to look for the faces of George Washington and Abraham Lincoln in the rocks just down the road beneath Square Butte. They're even listed as a point of interest on her Navajo map.

Stopping at the pullout near Square Butte, a distinctive block of rock jutting upward from a mesa, I find the matching formations said to display the presidential profiles. But beyond that they lose me. While I can see the vague outline of faces, they could have easily named them after cartoon characters and been just as accurate. No one is going to confuse this spot for Mount Rushmore.

The road continues west as it curves around Square Butte—hey, that one I can totally see—and crosses open plains. The carved wall of White Mesa parallels the road to the south, punctuated with distinctive spires and hoodoos. It's a few more miles to Kaibito, a tiny settlement with a general store and not much else. Yet this is an important place to the Dinés. When the US Army was waging its war on the Navajos in 1863–1864, many families avoided capture by hiding in the lonely canyons of the Kaibito Plateau.

For the next several miles it's a long sweep of grasslands that are broken by big dollops of sandstone, like rock islands floating in a sea of high desert scrub.

Before entering Page, you'll pass two very crowded parking lots. This marks the access points for the Southwest's most famous slot canyon, Antelope Canyon. If you've seen the iconic photos of speared sunlight swaddled in red-orange tones of sandstone, that's Antelope Canyon. The narrow crevice is divided into two sections. The trail enters Upper Antelope through a slit in the cliffs. It's a short and easy path,

Travel Note Page has a relatively short history, established in 1957 as a housing camp for workers building Glen Canyon Dam.

embraced by swirls of pearl-smooth walls. Lower Antelope is longer but requires climbing ladders and steps. Tour guides are required for both. Multiple companies offer guided tours several times daily. Even though solitude may be in short supply, magic in these slender cathedrals of light and stone is plentiful.

The scenic road comes to a close when Arizona 98 dead-ends at US 89. But just because you've run out of road, doesn't mean you've run out of scenery. You're at the edge of Lake Powell. The possibilities are endless.

It's a living mirage—one of those pinch-me-I-must-be-dreaming sights. Surrounded by miles of inhospitable desert, water shimmers in the sun. The towering sandstone walls of Glen Canyon cradle this vast reservoir. Forget everything you thought you knew about lakes. The long sinuous jewel-like body of water stretches for 186 miles into Utah. Lake Powell features 1,960 miles of shoreline, more than the entire continental west coast of the United States. With so many side canyons filled there are countless nooks and crannies to be explored by boat. With the blues and greens of the lake contrasting with the scorched reds and soft oranges of the cliffs, this terrain matches even the Grand Canyon for displays of startling, soul-freeing color.

Technically, Lake Powell is a water-storage facility created when Glen Canyon Dam began corralling the waters of the Colorado River in 1963. You can rent all manner of watercraft from luxury houseboats to speedboats to kayaks from Antelope Point and Wahweap Marina. Scenic cruises are also offered.

Hiking

NAVAJO NATIONAL MONUMENT

If you don't have the time or stamina to hike to either of the large pueblos, the monument still offers some nice options. The Sandal Trail should be your first choice as it crosses a rock ledge leading to an overlook with a view of Betatakin framed in its sandstone alcove. The paved trail is 1.3 miles round trip. The Aspen Trail (0.8 miles round trip) branches off the Sandal Trail and drops steeply through the forest to view a relic stand of aspen, habitat for the endangered Mexican spotted owl. Some stair climbing is required. Canyon View Trail skirts the head of Betatakin Canyon and leads to a historic ranger station. It's also 0.8 miles round trip. There is no admission fee to Navajo National Monument. (928) 672-2700, www.nps.gov/nava.

HORSESHOE BEND

Treat yourself to an optical thunderbolt just south of Page. A short 0.6-mile hike leads to Horseshoe Bend Overlook perched atop a steep cliff with the emerald-green Colorado River shimmering a thousand feet below. You'll have no trouble figuring out how this spot earned its name because the river makes a sweeping horseshoe-shaped curve. It is an eye-popping, jaw-dropping sight that has been made famous by social media posts. There is no shade and it can get ridiculously crowded, but it is still very much worth the effort. The trailhead is located off US 89, 2 miles south of Page. There is a parking fee. www.cityofpage.org/hsb.

RIM TRAIL

This ambitious pathway circles the perimeter of Manson Mesa, the high perch that holds the city of Page. It's mostly flat, easy walking with a few short grades but is also completely exposed. Four trailheads means you can reach a portion of the trail that stretches for several miles from just about anywhere in town, including North Lake Powell Blvd. behind McDonald's. Go for as long as you like and enjoy some impressive views of Lake Powell and the surrounding desert. (928) 645-9496, www.visitpagelake powell.com.

Where to Eat and Sleep

AMIGO CAFÉ, KAYENTA

Located in downtown Kayenta, near the intersection of US 160 (they don't even bother listing their street address), Amigo Café dishes up some of the best food you'll find on the Navajo Nation. Their hearty breakfasts will get your day started right. They combine Mexican dishes with Navajo favorites, and everything is fresh and flavorful with just the right hints of spiciness. Don't worry, there are a few American items on the menu too for the non-adventurous. They've been in business since 1983, which tells you they're doing something very right. US 163, (928) 697-8448.

DAM BAR & GRILLE, PAGE

A 30-foot etched glass wall and scaled-down Glen Canyon Dam are not your typical restaurant décor, but this is Page, the town that exists because of the dam and the lake that came after. Lunch menu features sandwiches, salads, pizzas, and burgers—and they roll out the steaks for dinner. There's bar seating and restaurant booths, and they pride themselves on serving the coldest beer in town. There's also a patio to enjoy. 644 N. Navajo Dr., (928) 645-2161, www.damplaza.com.

LAKE POWELL MOTEL, PAGE

A quaint, family-owned motel conveniently located in downtown Page, walking distance to restaurants and shops. Choose from one- and two-bedroom apartments that come with living rooms and full kitchens. They also offer a motel suite that's easy on the budget. There's no pool or fancy lobby. The motel is designed for travelers who want a comfortable place to relax but came to this part of the state to explore, not lounge around poolside. 750 S. Navajo Dr., (480) 452-9895, www.lakepowellmotel.net.

MOENKOPI LEGACY INN & SUITES, TUBA CITY

Opened in 2010, this attractive hotel pays homage to Hopi villages with its use of color, symbols, and pueblo-style architecture. The spacious rooms are comfortable and quiet. Guests enjoy a heated pool and complimentary but limited breakfast. They also offer tours of the Hopi villages and landscape, providing access to places where unaccompanied visitors can't go. 1 Legacy Ln., (928) 283-4500, www.experiencehopi .com.

When You Go

Navajo National Monument: (928) 672-2700, www.nps.gov/nava.

Visit Page Lake Powell: 6 N. Lake Powell Blvd., (928) 645-9496, www.visit pagelakepowell.com.

Antelope Canyon: Fee. (928) 645-0268, www.navajonationparks.org.

Glen Canyon National Recreation Area: Fee. (928) 608-6200, www.nps.gov/glca.

Antelope Point Marina: Fee. (928) 645-5900, www.antelopepointlakepowell.com.

Wahweap Marina: (928) 645-1027, www .lakepowellmarinas.com.

CENTRAL HIGHLANDS

Woodland Lake Park offers a quick and easy getaway in the middle of Pinetop-Lakeside. Photo by the author.

White River Scenic Road

Overview A short journey through a ponderosa pine forest and river canyons provides an introduction to the rich cultural history of the White Mountain Apache Tribe.

Route Numbers Arizona State Highway 73.

Mileage The scenic road is 10.87 miles (Milepost 346.85 to Milepost 357.72).

Special Notes The road is entirely on the Fort Apache Indian Reservation, sometimes called the White Mountain Reservation. It connects to White Mountain Scenic Road.

The White Mountains are about as far from desert as it gets in Arizona. That's a big part of their allure when temperatures begin to rise in the low country. Surrounded by dense forest at 7,200 feet and ringed by sparkling lakes, Pinetop–Lakeside makes the perfect base camp to explore the region.

They were once separate communities but over the years have grown together to form one long thin town. And even that's been widened to include Show Low, inching over from the western edge. Visitors will find a great selection of lodging, restaurants, and shops. But no one travels to this high mountain getaway to linger indoors. It's time to get out and explore.

Drive southeast of Pinetop for just a few miles to Hon-Dah Resort Casino, operated by the White Mountain Apache Tribe. Hon-Dah means "welcome" or "be my guest" in Apache. At this junction, Arizona 73 turns south marking the beginning of the scenic road. The highway meanders through the ponderosa pines down a canyon alongside the North Fork of White River.

Cooley Mountain looms to the east. The peak is named for Corydon E. Cooley, a scout for General George Crook during the campaign against the Apache. Cooley, who had two Apache wives, was also responsible for one of Arizona's most curiously named towns. Legend has it that Cooley and a former partner played cards to settle a dispute over a large mountain ranch. The game dragged on for hours and finally the weary card player said, "Show low and you win." Cooley turned over the two of clubs, winning the game and the ranch, which became the town of Show Low. That also explains how the main street through Show Low is named Deuce of Clubs.

About 4 miles south of Hon-Dah, a dirt road leads to the Williams Creek National Fish Hatchery. A few miles farther down 73 is the signed turnoff for the Alchesay National Fish Hatchery. These two stations played an important role in saving the native Apache trout, Arizona's state fish. The White Mountain Apache Tribe was way out in front on the conservation efforts. When it became apparent the last remaining pure populations of Apache trout lived in the streams high on Mount Baldy, they closed the area to sport fishing. They developed a brood stock of Apache trout and began raising them at the hatcheries. Rainbow, brook, and brown trout are also produced for stocking in tribal waters all over the Southwest. Due to those successful efforts, the numbers of Apache trout continue to grow, their range has been expanded, and even limited fishing has been permitted. Visitors can tour both hatcheries.

The Alchesay hatchery is named for the most revered of the White Mountain Apache chiefs. As a scout for the US Army in the 1870s, Alchesay was awarded the Congressional Medal of Honor for his gallantry in the brutal Tonto Basin campaign.

Early on, the White Mountain Apaches chose not to go to war against the white settlers flooding the area. Instead they provided scouts and helped fight hostile tribes like the Tonto and Chiricahua Apaches that they traditionally fought anyway.

Travel Note Alchesay's grave is located to the west of Arizona 73, between the turnoffs for the two fish hatcheries.

The scenic road officially ends near the turnoff for the Alchesay National Fish Hatchery, which strikes me as weird because there's still so much good stuff to see. Keep driving south and soon you're entering the town of Whiteriver, headquarters of the Fort Apache Indian Reservation. The actual White River wends its way through a steep-sided gorge at the edge of town.

It's just a few miles farther to Fort Apache, where so much history unfolded. During the turbulent years of the Indian Wars, Fort Apache served as a key post for the army campaign. Established in 1870 as Camp Ord, it was meant to guard the White Mountain Agency. When famed Indian fighter George Crook was named commander of the Department of Arizona, he believed it would take Apaches to catch Apaches. He recruited fifty White Mountain Apaches, and even went so far as to pay them the same as his white scouts, much to the dismay of his superiors. But it would prove to be a decisive gamble as it allowed him to wage a relentless campaign, dogging each renegade band that refused to accept life on the reservation. The bloody era finally ended in 1886 when Geronimo surrendered in Skeleton Canyon in Southern Arizona.

The military presence continued at Fort Apache until 1922, when the facilities were converted into a boarding school. When it closed, Fort Apache was the only remaining non-mechanized military post in the United States.

Today, over twenty buildings, dating from the 1870s through the 1930s, comprise a 288-acre historic park. Visitors can take a self-guided walking tour through the fort.

A band of wild horses keeps a wary eye in the forests around Show Low, Pinetop, and Lakeside. Photo by the author.

Start at the White Mountain Apache Cultural Center and Museum where they celebrate the Apache heritage. Permanent and temporary exhibits, historic photographs, and artifacts are all part of the experience. A few miles away, the Kinishba Ruins National Historic Landmark protects the remains of a large village occupied by the ancestors of the Hopi and Zuni people from about AD 1200 to 1400. Adolph Bandelier, anthropological explorer of the Southwest, was the first Anglo to write about the site in 1892. Visitors to the ruins must check in at the museum at Fort Apache. Admission to the museum and park includes access to the ruins.

After visiting Kinishba you can turn around and return the way you came or continue on 73, which is what I opt to do. By this point the road has begun to ramble northwest. The basin is surrounded by green hills and rough meadows punctuated with juniper and pinion pine. In just over 20 miles Arizona 73 will end at US 60 in the small community of Carrizo.

A left turn will send you dropping down through the rugged Salt River Canyon to

Travel Note When the fort closed, the Apache scouts were reassigned to other posts with most going to Fort Huachuca in southeastern Arizona. There they served primarily as game rangers on the post until the last scouts retired in 1947.

Globe (63 miles). A right turn will climb back to the Mogollon Rim, 24 miles to Show Low. There are still a couple of spectacular scenic roads waiting to be driven across the White Mountains.

Hiking

WOODLAND LAKE PARK

For a gentle stretch of your legs in a peaceful setting and a chance to spot wildlife, just head to downtown Lakeside. To be honest, there is no downtown Lakeside, since the town is just strung along Arizona 260. Yet Woodland Lake Park still serves as a central core and gathering spot for the community. The 583-acre park includes picnic tables, grills, playgrounds, ball fields, and a 1.25-mile paved path circling the luscious little lake. The nonprofit White Mountain Nature Center is part of the park, and they can provide additional information and let you know about any programs being conducted during your stay. 425 S. Woodland Rd., (928) 358-3069, www.whitemountain naturecenter.org.

TIMBER MESA TRAIL #636

This is a piece of the trail system developed by TRACKS, a volunteer group that works with the forest service and White Mountain communities. They've built over 200 miles of interconnected, well-marked pathways. The trail scrambles to the top of a butte and then makes a loop through the forest. While tracing the mesa's rocky edge, the trees break apart providing nice panoramas of the meadows below, the wetlands of Jacques Marsh and Pinetop–Lakeside. The loop is 7.5 miles total. As a bonus, walk one hundred yards up the fire road from the parking lot to find twin stone chimneys, the remnants of historic Jacques Ranch, and some informational signage. Look for the signed trailhead off Porter Mountain Road in Lakeside. (928) 368-6700, Ext. 3, www.trackswhitemountains.org.

SPRINGS TRAIL #633

This is a sweet loop (3.6 miles) through sun-dappled pine forest that also crisscrosses low-lying riparian areas. The terrain stays level and neither Billy Creek nor Thompson Creek present a challenge, making this a good hike for kids. Summer wildflowers add a sprinkling of color. This is also a good area to spot wildlife drawn by the creeks and stock tanks in the pasture. The trailhead is off Sky Hi Road in Pinetop. (928) 368-6700, Ext. 3, www.trackswhite mountains.org.

Where to Eat and Stay

THE HOUSE, SHOW LOW

Stop by and it feels like you're at a friend's backyard barbecue. The wood-paneled building is simple inside and framed by a patio. Out back is a grassy lawn with picnic tables, a cornhole board, and a yard bar—sort of a cross between a saloon and a tree house. Try the House Burger, a fresh patty topped with roasted poblano chili, fried onion strings, pepper jack cheese, and chipotle aioli—a nice combo of textures and flavors, crunchy with a little spice on the back end. 1191 E. Hall St., (928) 537-9273, www.thehouseshowlow.com.

ARROWHEAD CAFÉ & MARKETPLACE, FORT APACHE

The Arrowhead Café & Marketplace should be one of the must stops on your walking tour of historic Fort Apache. Located on Officers' Row, the cheerful café serves a creative menu of sandwiches, wraps, and tacos, along with some traditional dishes. Vegetables are grown at the local reservation farm. Manned by young people, Arrowhead provides youth entrepreneurial programs for the Native community. 103 General Crook St., (928)338-4278, www.arrowheadcafe.com.

WHISPERING PINES, PINETOP

The cabins at Whispering Pines are spread across thirteen acres of mixed timber abutting the national forest. It creates a nice backwoods feel, yet shopping and restaurants are surprisingly close. Choose from studio cabins; one-, two-, or three-bedroom units; deluxe spa cabins; and even an elegant Victorian. This is an older property with a lot of charm. Cabins are well maintained, fully furnished, carpeted, and stocked with firewood. With over three-dozen cabins, you can easily find one that fits your budget and family needs. 237 E. White Mountain Blvd., (800) 840-3867, www.whisperingpinesaz.com.

When You Go

Pinetop–Lakeside Chamber of Commerce: 518 W. Mountain Blvd. Lakeside, (928) 367-4290, www.pinetoplakesidechamber.com.

Show Low Chamber of Commerce: 81 E. Deuce of Clubs, (928) 537-2326, www.showlowchamber.com.

Hon-Dah Resort Casino: 777 Arizona 260, (800) 929-8744, www.hon-dah.com.

White Mountain Apache Office of Tourism: (928) 338-4346, www.whitemountainapache.org.

White Mountain Apache Game and Fish: Outdoor activities on Fort Apache Indian Reservation require permits. (928) 338-4385, www.wmatoutdoor.org.

Alchesay–Williams Creek National Fish Hatchery Complex: (Williams Creek) (928) 334-2346, (Alchesay) (928) 338-4901, www.fws.gov/southwest/fisheries/awc.

White Mountain Apache Cultural Center and Museum: Fee. (928) 338-4625.

White Mountain Scenic Road

Overview This high country loop sweeps past sparkling lakes, crosses trout-filled rivers, and traverses meadows and forests on the flanks of mighty mountains. It's deliriously green in the summer, a blaze of color in the fall, and a snowy wonderland in winter.

Route Numbers Arizona State Highways 260, 261, and 273.

Mileage The scenic road is 67.3 miles (Milepost 360.77 to Milepost 393.03, Milepost 393.8 to Milepost 412.5, and Milepost 377.46 to Milepost 393.8).

Special Notes A portion of the road crosses the Fort Apache Indian Reservation. It connects to White River Scenic Road and Coronado Trail National Scenic Byway. Winter weather conditions can pose travel problems. Both Arizona 261 and Arizona 273 close during the winter. The 4-mile-long portion of 273 from Arizona 260 to Sunrise Park remains open to provide access to the ski area.

From Pinetop, Arizona 260 heads east and quickly reaches Hon-Dah Resort Casino. From here Arizona 73 turns south, the White River Scenic Road, but for this adventure continue traveling east on 260 across the Fort Apache Indian Reservation. The road soon passes through the small settlement of McNary. This was once the site of a thriving sawmill, but it burned down in 1979 and was never rebuilt. Since then McNary has largely faded back into the pines.

A few miles east of town, lush meadows replace portions of the forest. This is what makes this the quintessential White Mountains drive, a combination of meadow and forest all drenched in vivid shades of green. And of course, lakes at every turn. You can't throw a rock in the White Mountains without hearing a splash.

Horses graze in pastures near the junction with Arizona 473, the turnoff for Hawley Lake. They look fat and sassy enjoying the bounty of luxuriant grass and cooperative rains. If you're looking for a little side trip, it's a 9-mile drive climbing through a forest of aspen, pine, spruce, and fir on a

Travel Note Hawley Lake gained notoriety on a January day in 1971 when temperatures plummeted to a bone-chilling 40 degrees below zero. That's the coldest temperature ever recorded in Arizona.

paved road to reach Hawley Lake. There's a campground, lodge, rustic cabins, and store at the lake, although hours may be limited.

You'll soon reach the turnoff to Horseshoe Cienega. It's only a mile down a dirt road to the elegant curved lake of 121 acres. This is a great fishing spot for those with limited mobility. Some anglers simply back their cars up to the water's edge and set up lawn chairs. There's a small campground and store. Remember, permits from the White Mountain Apache Tribe are required for fishing, camping, hiking, biking, or other outdoor activities.

Back on 260, the road continues to rise through dense groves of aspens and pines. Intimate A-1 Lake sits just off the highway, ringed by trees, at an elevation of 8,900 feet. That always surprises me because it never feels like the road is climbing quite so much. It's named for Apache chief Alchesay, who was awarded the Congressional Medal of Honor as an Army scout. His name proved difficult for US Army officials to pronounce, so they simply referred to him as A-1.

This would be a beautiful drive in the fall as well with so many big stands of aspen shimmering in the breeze. The road tops out amid wide rocky meadows surrounding a junction with Arizona 273, the turnoff for Sunrise Park Resort. I'll utilize this road on the return. The big timber that had been prominent for much of the journey is now

One stretch of the White Mountain Scenic Road crosses dramatic high-country meadows. Photo by the author.

Aptly named Big Lake is one of the many bodies of water spread across the White Mountains. Photo by the author.

just a light fringe around the edges of the grasslands. Cattle graze alongside what appears to be the skeletons of billboards but are actually snow fences enjoying their summer break.

Expansive meadows are the norm for the rest of 260 heading into Springerville and Eagar. I soon pass Arizona 373, the road to the isolated little hamlet of Greer. Then the road descends, dropping into the Round Valley. Although softly benign now, these grassy hills are old cinder cones, part of the Springerville volcanic field that stretches 1,200 square miles across the landscape. Some of the hills are streaked by dark gashes, wounds where rough cinders spill from their flanks. On more than one occasion I've seen bighorn sheep grazing contentedly on the shoulders of these once explosive hills.

Sitting on the valley floor, Eagar lies just ahead. It's a picturesque community with its tidy ranches and homes set along the winding curves of the Little Colorado River. Like Pinetop–Lakeside, Springerville and Eagar have grown together to form a single entity, although they work hard to retain their respective identities. Locals always know the boundary line between the two towns, but visitors would be hard-pressed to figure it out. No matter. They are lovely communities, small friendly ranching towns with food, gas, lodging, and a couple of interesting museums.

Meanwhile, the official scenic road turns south onto Arizona 261 about 3 miles before reaching Eagar. It crosses the Little Colorado and immediately begins to climb, through heavy juniper woods early and then into the ponderosa pines. At the highest elevations evidence of the 2011 Wallow Fire can be seen. I pull over at the Point of the Mountain Scenic Overlook with restrooms, picnic tables, and a viewing platform with interpretive signs. The hillsides below are blanketed in thistle, Mexican hats, penstemons, and assorted other summer blooms.

Past the overlook, Arizona 261 cuts a long line across high meadows the rest of the way. These are top-of-the-world meadows. Trees are marginalized, chased beyond the horizon by a galloping prairie. A wild canopy of blue drapes above the expanse. Earth and sky seem perfectly matched in this place, and I am a lone vertical note connected to both. Standing in the grass I am filled with the wild thought that I'm the only thing propping up the sky and when I leave it will collapse into the embrace of these soft plains. Then I thought, who am I to get in the way of true love? What's meant to be, will be. I drove on.

The road ends at the junction with Arizona 273 at Crescent Lake, a lovely little body of water filling a shallow basin. Continue south for 3 miles to Big Lake. With a surface area of 450 acres stocked with rainbow, brook, and cutthroat trout, in addition to five campgrounds, and ringed by a swath of forest, this is one of the most popular lakes in the White Mountains.

After leaving Big Lake, head northwest on Arizona 273, the final segment of the White Mountain Scenic Road. It climbs from meadows into mixed timber with just a few light burn scars visible. Then the road begins to drop into picturesque Lee Valley. I spotted the East Baldy Trailhead (see Hiking) and quickly pulled over just to stretch my legs for a mile or two.

A storm was gathering, and I ambled up the trail through a lanky meadow along the banks of the East Fork of the Little Colorado River into the trees. At 11,420 feet, Mount Baldy is the highest peak in the White Mountains and is held sacred by the Apache people. I had a pleasant jaunt and was returning to my truck when I heard dogs howling from the forest over on the next ridge. It sounded like four or five of them, and they were really carrying on. I took a few more steps and stopped in my tracks. What would a pack of dogs be doing out here in the wilderness?

I realized suddenly that I was listening to wolves. This area is part of the Mexican Gray Wolf Reintroduction Program, designed to reintroduce the species back to their native habitat. I hadn't given it much thought, but now it seemed very real. The howling went on for several minutes mixed with a chorus of yips and barks. So I'm not sure what was going on, if it was a hunt, a fight, or a party. As far as I know, this was the first time in my life I had ever heard the beasts. I didn't see a thing but it's still one of my favorite animal encounters. I'll always remember standing beneath stormy skies amid the aspens and wildflowers on the slope of a sacred mountain listening to wolf howls shatter the silence. Now that's a summer day to remember in Arizona.

The road continues past Lee Valley Lake. At 9,400 feet it's Arizona's highest lake. And I'm soon passing Sunrise Park Resort. During winter the slopes of Sunrise Mountain are teeming with skiers and snowboarders. But in summer they roll out a playground full of high-flying, fast-moving, and bouncy thrills. You can ride the scenic chairlift to the 10,700-foot summit. Or if

Travel Note Although they once numbered in the thousands, wolves were wiped out in the US by the mid-1970s with just a handful existing in zoos. The Mexican Gray Wolf Reintroduction Program has created a small but growing population of lobos in the mountains of Eastern Arizona and Western New Mexico.

The brilliant hues of changing aspen leaves attract visitors to the White Mountains each autumn. Courtesy of Mike Koopsen, Sedona.

that's too slow-paced, take Arizona's longest zip-line tour soaring high above the pine trees for over a mile. There's also the 300-foot tubing slide, airbag jumps, and downhill mountain biking.

Four miles past Sunrise, Arizona 273 ends at Arizona 260. Turn left to return to Pinetop–Lakeside (29 miles), or hang a right to go to Springerville–Eagar (21 miles).

More Scenic Driving

Arizona 373 is a stubby little stretch of pavement, only 3 miles long, but it winds through a pretty nice neighborhood as it passes a handful of lakes and reservoirs, then ends at the village of Greer. Nestled in a high mountain valley, Greer offers an ideal escape from the clamor of civilization, although there are cabins, a lodge, and a couple of restaurants. Not many towns have a trout stream as the main drag, but that's just how things are done in Greer. The Little Colorado River cuts through the middle of town flanked by green meadows that lap at the base of forested slopes. Sitting at 8,525 feet means four distinct seasons. Greer is especially known for mild summers and snowy winters. Many of the surrounding hiking trails become cross-country ski routes.

Hiking

EAST BALDY TRAIL #95

Two trails climb the slopes of Mount Baldy, one following the West Fork of the Little Colorado River (West Baldy) and this one following the East Fork. They both are 7 miles one way and meet near the top. The actual summit is on the Fort Apache Indian Reservation and is off-limit to non-tribal members. Please respect their laws. It's a spectacular trail crossing meadows and climbing through big stands of mixed conifers and a curious collection of boulders. Keep an ear and eye peeled for wolves. Trailhead is off Arizona 273, 11 miles south of Arizona 260. (928) 333-6200, www.fs.usda.gov/asnf.

RAILROAD GRADE TRAIL #601

Since it stretches for 21 miles, don't plan on tackling the entire trail. But it does make an easy introduction to some of the best parts of the White Mountains. It's part of the "Rails to Trails" program designed to preserve America's old railroad network by converting them into trails and offers panoramic views and level grades. Look for the signed trailhead on the south side of Arizona 260, 1.5 miles east of Arizona 273. There's another trailhead at Big Lake. (928) 333-6200, www.fs.usda.gov/asnf.

RIVER WALK TRAIL

This easy half-mile stroll along the twisting curves of the Little Colorado River is a great spot to watch animals going about their business. From the stoplight in Springerville, go 1 mile west on US 60 to the parking lot on the left. Watch for beavers and mule deer along the riparian corridor as the skinny river winds among trees and cattails, while pronghorn, coyote, and prairie dog favor the surrounding grasslands. And of course, birds of all varieties are plentiful. It's part of the Becker Lake Wildlife Area. As a bonus hike, the Lakeview Trail makes a mile loop to a viewing platform along the edge of Becker Lake.

Where to Eat and Stay

GOOB'S PIZZA, SPRINGERVILLE

There's a nice retro vibe to this mom-and-pop eatery tucked away in a strip mall. This is the kind of pizza place you remember visiting after school to play video games and grab a slice. They make their dough fresh daily and splash on a generous portion of homemade sauce. Choose between thin crust and traditional hand tossed, and then slather on the fresh toppings. 211 S. Mountain Ave., (928) 333-1502.

REED'S LODGE, SPRINGERVILLE

This family-owned lodge dates back to 1949 but is well maintained, with large, clean rooms and lots of country charm. Guests will enjoy pine walls and beams, plenty of local art, and a courtyard brimming with flowers during summer months. The owners also offer several types of tours and outings. 514 E. Main St. (928) 333-4323, www.k5reeds.com.

When You Go

Pinetop–Lakeside Chamber of Commerce: 518 W. Mountain Blvd., Lakeside, (928) 367-4290, www.pinetoplakesidechamber.com.

Hon-Dah Resort Casino: 777 Arizona 260, (800) 929-8744, www.hon-dah.com.

White Mountain Apache Office of Tourism: (928) 338-4346, www.whitemountainapache.org.

White Mountain Apache Game and Fish: Outdoor activities on Fort Apache Indian Reservation require permits. (928) 338-4385, www.wmatoutdoor.org.

Springerville–Eagar Regional Chamber of Commerce: 7 W. Main St., Springerville, (928) 333-2123, www.springervilleeagarchamber.com.

Sunrise Park Resort: (855) 735-7669, www.sunriseskiparkaz.com.

Greer: www.greerarizona.com.

Coronado Trail National Scenic Byway

Overview This long, winding, and seldom-traveled highway begins in a grassy valley near the Little Colorado River, climbs across the White Mountains, and drops through a rugged canyon past a huge open-pit mine. Most of the drive travels through long slender Greenlee County along the New Mexico border.

Route Numbers US Highway 191 and US Highway 180.

Mileage The scenic byway is 102.67 miles (Milepost 406 to Milepost 426.93, and Milepost 172 to Milepost 253.74).

Special Notes Hundreds of curves and mountain grades make this a challenging but rewarding drive. Services and cell-phone reception are extremely limited. The road can be traveled year-round but may be temporarily closed because of heavy snow in winter. It connects to the White Mountain Scenic Road.

As a shortcut, the Coronado Trail is an abject failure.

Anyone in a hurry should give the twisted stretch of highway a wide berth. This is a meandering, moseying, slow-motion drive. The 123 miles of pavement between Springerville and Clifton features 460 curves as it skirts the eastern edge of the Apache–Sitgreaves Forest. Thrilling and dramatic, yes, but speedy it's not.

The road is narrow and winding, dipping from one curve to the next, perfect for motorcycles and high-performance sports cars. Or for rattling old pickup trucks with galaxies of miles and squeaky brakes, which is what I drive. All you need to tackle this undulating python of pavement is time on your hands and a desire to experience a stunning swath of Arizona.

The segment of US 191 known as the Coronado Trail National Scenic Byway cuts through verdant forests and alpine meadows before dropping from the heights of the White Mountains to cactus-dotted deserts below. Francisco Vázquez de Coronado followed a similar route as he searched for the "Seven Cities of Cibola" more than 450 years ago. The road roughly parallels the New Mexico border and claims the distinction of being the curviest and least-traveled federal highway in the country.

I started in the conjoined towns of Springerville–Eagar. Nestled in the Round Valley at an elevation of 7,000 feet, Springerville and Eagar are ranching communities with a storied past. Ike Clanton, who survived the shootout at the OK Corral in Tombstone, wasn't so lucky in Springerville. He was gunned down by a lawman in 1887 while trying to avoid arrest for cattle rustling. Casa Malpais, a renowned archaeological site constructed of volcanic rock dating back to AD 1250, sits at the edge of town.

Allow yourself a day to visit area museums, fish in nearby lakes, or take in a film at Arizona's oldest movie theater, the El Rio, opened in 1915. Springerville also contains a Madonna of the Trail statue, one of a series of twelve monuments constructed in the 1920s along the National Old Trails Road.

Pulling out of the Round Valley, the road immediately begins to climb. The highway makes long, lazy bends through a checkerboard of timber and pasture. It curls along the edge of Nelson Reservoir, a shimmering lake lapping against grassy hills. Stocked

---

Travel Note Hollywood icon John Wayne once owned the 26 Bar Ranch on the mountain slopes above Eagar and was a frequent visitor to the area. The town holds its annual John Wayne Days event each summer to celebrate the cowboy way of life.

Boaters enjoy a summer day on Luna Lake near Alpine. Photo by the author.

with rainbow, brown, and brook trout, Nelson is a popular spot for local anglers. There are picnic tables, restrooms, and a boat ramp.

The road passes through the small community of Nutrioso, settled by Mormons in the 1870s. To the east, the rising bulk of Escudilla Mountain fills the skyline. At 10,912 feet, this is Arizona's third-highest mountain (see Hiking).

After crossing the Alpine Divide, the highway drops down a narrow canyon toward one of the region's most picturesque towns. Reminiscent of a Swiss village, Alpine sits near the headwaters of the San Francisco River, ringed by mountains. It serves as a base camp for outdoor recreation—hunting, fishing, hiking, biking, and cross-country skiing. There's even a high-elevation golf course.

As downtowns go, Alpine is small but welcoming, with a handful of businesses strung along the crossroads of US 191 and US 180. You can stroll down the sidewalk to grab a burger, a beer, a slice of homemade pie, and some bait, and that's really all the civilization you need for an idyllic summer getaway. Be sure to gas up before you leave town. It will be many miles before you have another chance.

About 2 miles south of Alpine, I get my first real peek at damage from the 2011 Wallow Fire. Entire mountainsides are stubbled with blackened tree trunks. The heartbreaking scene continues uninterrupted for the next few miles and then pulls back. Wallow was a wind-driven fire resulting in a mosaic of damage across a widespread area. While the scars remain visible for many miles to come, it becomes spottier. And already

Petroglyphs are etched into a rocky cliff face at Sipe White Mountain Wildlife Area. Photo by the author.

verdant grasses and tall aspen saplings fill the scarred terrain. Life goes on.

Even if you're not spending the night at Hannagan Meadow Lodge, stop for a bite in their restaurant or just to stretch your legs and sniff the cool mountain air. Oxygen at 9,100 feet just seems to have a fragrance all its own. Hannagan Meadow Lodge was built after the dedication of the "Clifton to Springerville" road in 1926. During the ceremony, the new road was referred to as the "Trail of Coronado," and the nickname stuck.

Below Hannagan Meadow, the curves sharpen, twisting through forests for 6 miles until reaching Blue Vista. This sweeping overlook is perched at the edge of the Mogollon Rim some 4,000 feet above the valleys below. Far-ranging views stretch across lines of mountains that roll towards the horizon in waves. A bluish haze paints the ridges, and I'm struck by how much the panorama reminds me of Tennessee's Great Smoky Mountains National Park. Just when I think I have Arizona figured out, it throws me a curve. Lots of them, actually.

Travel Note The Wallow Fire was started in the summer of 2011 by two careless campers and torched nearly 540,000 acres. It was the largest wildfire in Arizona history.

From the outlook the road slithers down the mountainside. Narrow switchbacks drop from the heights, weaving through miles of dense forests. Along the way are numerous picnic areas, hiking trails, and campgrounds. It would be easy to lose a week exploring these parts.

After a while it becomes difficult to distinguish where one curve ends and another begins. At one point the road unkinks and runs straight as an arrow, and I expect to experience a bout of vertigo from the non-curviness as it slices through golden grasslands. But it's only a momentary blip, and the twisties start back up as I slice through woodlands and climb up and over green ridges. For many years, the road was US 666 and known as the Devil's Highway. No doubt it's been called much worse by kids prone to carsickness.

Finally, the road tumbles down the steep-sided canyon of Chase Creek, defined by angular stone formations and craggy slopes. Soon afterward I climb past the fabled Morenci Mine, one of the largest man-made holes in the world. While I wouldn't go so far as to call an open pit scenic, the Morenci Mine is impressive. The massive complex extends for several miles, the deep pits ribbed by long sculpted benches. Big trucks can be seen as small specks rumbling in and out of the multi-hued depths. There are a couple of overlooks where you can get a closer look at Arizona's largest copper mine.

Past the company town of Morenci, which seems bustling, I reach the last stop of the Coronado Trail. Clifton is spackled into the seams of the rocky canyon with a beautiful collection of historic homes and buildings. Long before technological advancements led to the open-pit behemoth up the road, Clifton developed during underground mining in the late 1800s. It

> **Travel Note** Keep an eye peeled for the resident herd of bighorn sheep often seen in and around Clifton.

wears the scars of its boom-and-bust lifestyle, not to mention the numerous floods that ravaged the narrow defile.

Clifton reminds me of Bisbee, another mining town that had to reinvent itself. A few decades ago only a handful of shops and galleries were open in Bisbee, perched in the Mule Mountains southwest of Clifton. Both towns share the same precariously perched architecture, the same historic foundations with lots of potential. Bisbee went on to blossom into a thriving arts community with a decidedly quirky vibe. Right now only a few shops and restaurants are open in Clifton, along with the small but interesting Greenlee Historical Museum. But I have a good feeling about the little burg. I look forward to seeing Clifton flourish in coming years as more artistic types discover the town.

This marks the end of the Coronado Trail. US 191 continues south to Douglas, but it's time for me to turn off in Safford and make the long drive home. Come to think of it, Safford is a town I've been meaning to explore. And after all, it's not like I'm in a hurry.

Watch for wildlife while traveling the Coronado Trail, including elk, deer, and pronghorn antelope, the fastest land mammal in North America. Courtesy of Mike Koopsen, Sedona.

Hiking

SIPE WHITE MOUNTAIN WILDLIFE AREA

A few miles southeast of Eagar on 191, this 1,362-acre property offers a handful of short trails rambling through a range of habitats, along with historic cultural sites and an educational visitor center. The Arizona Game and Fish Department manages Sipe White Mountain Wildlife Area. The best birding is along the Rudd Creek Loop Trail, 3 miles of mostly flat terrain. The High Point Trail (1 mile) makes a moderate climb to several wildlife viewing overlooks with benches and one with a 20X spotting scope so you can scan the meadows below. (928) 367-4281.

ESCUDILLA MOUNTAIN TRAIL #308

A climb to the broad summit of Arizona's third-highest mountain offers spectacular views and a study in how wildfire impacts the landscape. The 2.9-mile out-and-back trail starts amid a dense grove of aspens. This forest, once heavy with fir and pine, was severely burned in a 1951 wildfire. Fast-growing aspens moved in, making this a popular spot for fall color. Sadly, the Wallow Fire swept across the upper reaches of Escudilla, causing widespread damage, although the lower slopes were left intact. Today, the high-burn scars are being healed by native grasses and aspen saplings, growing amid the eerie stands of scorched trunks. It's intriguing to see the various stages of recovery. The Escudilla Wilderness can be accessed via Forest Road 56, about 3 miles south of Nutrioso. (928) 339-5000, www.fs.usda.gov/asnf.

LUNA LAKE

The forests around Alpine are filled with lakes and streams, but Luna is the town's personal watery playground. A seventy-five-acre impoundment of the San Francisco River, Luna Lake supports a healthy population of rainbow and cutthroat trout. There are boat and canoe rentals, a ramp with paved parking, and picnic areas with gazebos. The campground sprawls amid a shady stand of ponderosa pines and two hiking/biking trails circle the lake. Located 3 miles east of Alpine on US 180.

Where to Eat and Stay

FOXFIRE AT ALPINE

Foxfire at Alpine occupies a historic home that's been beautifully redesigned. The warm contemporary décor includes a sculptural slate wall and the work of local artists on display. A few tables fill the dining room and others are on the screened-in front porch, which makes a lovely dining spot on a summer evening in the high country. Foxfire specializes in pizzas with a zesty homemade sauce, pastas, sandwiches, and salads. They also feature a surprisingly robust wine list. 42661 US 180, (928) 339-4344, www.foxfireatalpineaz.com.

HANNAGAN MEADOW LODGE

Built in 1926, Hannagan Meadow Lodge features a handful of rooms and ten rustic cabins scattered in the timber. Each room and cabin is adorned with antiques. You'll have homemade quilts, fireplaces, and rocking chairs but no television, telephone, or cell service—a sweet trade-off for a few days. 23150 US 191, (928) 339-4370, www.hannaganmeadow.com.

When You Go

Springerville–Eagar Regional Chamber of Commerce: 7 W. Main St., Springerville, (928) 333-2123, www.springervilleeagarchamber.com.

Casa Malpais: Fee. (928) 333-5375, www.casamalpais.org.

Alpine Chamber of Commerce: (928) 339-4330, www.alpinearizona.com.

Greenlee County Chamber of Commerce: 809 SE Old West Highway, Duncan, (928) 965-7943, www.greenleechamber.com.

Clifton: www.visitcliftonaz.com.

Desert to Tall Pines Scenic Road

Overview This winding mountain road travels to one of Arizona's most remote communities and through one of the bloodiest chapters of her history.

Route Numbers Forest Road 512, Arizona State Highway 288.

Mileage The scenic road is 76.3 miles (Milepost 0 to Milepost 23, and Milepost 311 to Milepost 257.7). It's 128 miles from Payson to Globe.

Special Notes Much of the road is unpaved and should not be attempted in inclement weather. Some sections include mountain grades and steep drop-offs. Services are limited, and cellphone reception is spotty.

This may be the most poetic moniker worn by any of the official scenic roads. It would also make an excellent state motto. Desert to tall pines hints at the diversity of Arizona. For folks living in the Phoenix valley, it serves as a weekend mantra as they flee the dragon-breath days of summer for cooler forested climes.

A word of caution before starting out: this is not a drive to take on a whim. Much of the road is unpaved. It's steep and narrow in places, and guardrails are nonexistent. The only services along the route are in Young. So pack food and water, and make sure the gas tank is full.

It will take a few hours to complete the journey. Along the way you'll enjoy a wide range of scenery, visit one of Arizona's most remote communities, and—as strange as it seems in this bucolic setting—pass through a chapter of bloody history. It all sounds like a day well spent.

Despite the cool name, I prefer to make the drive in reverse order, dropping from tall pines into the embrace of the desert. It feels natural somehow and ends with a flourish of dramatic scenery, including vistas of Roosevelt Lake and Four Peaks.

Start out in the ponderosa pine forests of the Mogollon Rim between Payson and Heber. From Arizona 260, 33 miles east of Payson, turn south on Forest Road 512 to begin the drive. You'll pass a perky little grove of aspens and plenty more pines. After 3 miles the pavement ends. That will continue for the length of the journey: sporadic stretches of asphalt interrupted by long sections of graded dirt. The road can be traveled in a sedan but should not be attempted when it's wet. Of course, you'll be more comfortable in a high-clearance vehicle. That also gives you the option to

Lavish sunsets are regular occurrences in the Sonoran Desert of Arizona. Photo by the author.

Visitors to the town of Young will find a handful of current businesses mingled with remnants of past eras. Photo by the author.

explore many of the side roads that meander to distant corners of the mountains. For example, where the pavement ends a road branches to the right leading to the Colcord Lookout Tower (3 miles), which affords some stunning views.

For the next several miles, the road travels through heavy forest. Sightings of elk and deer are common. This region provides habitat for mountain lion, bear, javelina, turkey, and many other species. There are campgrounds up and down the route and plenty of at-large sites. Camping is permitted only within 300 feet of the road. Since this is bear country, take all necessary precautions.

When the road breaks free of the timber curling down a ridgeline, you'll be treated to far-reaching vistas. The remoteness of the area becomes immediately apparent with the sight of forested mountains stretching into the distance. The Mazatzal Mountains rise to the west and the Sierra Ancha to the east. You won't find any signs of civilization until you approach Young. Pavement briefly resumes and FR 512 ends. You're now on Arizona 288.

If Young isn't exactly the town that time forgot, it's certainly one that stopped taking time's calls. Nestled in a grassy basin, ringed by taller peaks, Young, once known as Pleasant Valley, retains its cowtown charm. Electricity didn't arrive in the valley until 1965. Only a handful of businesses are scattered through town, including a couple of small markets—one with gas pumps, a restaurant or two, a ten-room motel, and a vineyard.

That peaceful feeling you experience as you enter the basin was not always the norm. This was the site of America's most savage feud, the ironically named Pleasant Valley War that lasted from 1882 to 1892. The Tewksburys and Grahams were former friends that had a falling out over cattle they jointly owned, and quite possibly rustled. The bitterness and accusations eventually ensnared friends, neighbors, lawmen, and hired guns.

When sheep were introduced into the valley in 1887, the violence exploded. The Tewksbury clan gave protection to a flock of sheep brought into the area. The Grahams attacked, killing a young Native American shepherd and driving off the animals. The Tewksburys retaliated and for the next five years gunfire echoed across the valley as ambushes and lynchings took place, each act seeming to prompt a bloodier response.

The war finally came to an end, not through any truce, but because there was nobody left to kill. In 1892 Tom Graham, who had sold his ranch to try and make a fresh start, was gunned down on the streets of Tempe by Ed Tewksbury. The Pleasant

Travel Note The Mogollon Rim is a soaring escarpment rising 2,000 feet in a sudden vertical thrust from the desert floor to the pine forests. It begins near the New Mexico border and slashes diagonally across Arizona to Sedona, defining the southern edge of the Colorado Plateau.

Valley War claimed between twenty and fifty lives, depending on whose account you believe. Both families were essentially wiped out. Ed Tewksbury went free (no one connected with the feud was ever found guilty), and there were no more Grahams to come gunning for him. It was literally a fight to the last man.

History buffs can visit some of the battle sites and graves of the victims. Five members of the Graham clan are buried in the Young cemetery. The grave of the Native American killed while tending his sheep can be found about a mile down Forest Road 200, just north of Young.

You'll soon lose the pavement heading south from Young. The road climbs into the hills, past a pullout at Pleasant Valley Vista (see Hiking). The views stretch for miles, giving you a chance to study this lush creek-watered basin that prompted so much bloodshed.

The road makes its way south through the pines past McFadden Peak and McFadden Horse Mountain. If you need a good leg stretch, you can hike Forest Road 561 to the top of McFadden Peak crowned with a lookout tower. It's less than 3 miles round trip with an elevation gain of almost 800 feet.

Workman Creek presents the possibility of an interesting detour. Forest Road 487 turns east alongside the stream that supports a nice crop of columbine and other wildflowers in late spring. But this is not a detour to be taken lightly. It's a narrow cliff-hugging road best suited for high-clearance vehicles, if not four-wheel drive. The payoff is a 200-foot waterfall spilling in a straight drop right beside the road.

It's about 3 miles to the falls. I was eager to see the cascade even though we were in the middle of a drought. I took it slow, and my biggest concern was meeting someone coming the other way because this is pretty much a one-laner with a steep drop down to the creek. Places to pull over are few, but you do pass three primitive camping areas.

Travel Note Pleasant Valley was renamed Young in 1890 after the area's first postmaster, Olla Beth Young.

I found a safe place to park and hiked the last half-mile to the falls, which was sadly little more than a lacy veil dropping to the creek below. Since I've seen photos of it, I know it's normally more robust. I'm glad I left my truck where I did as the road did take on a rougher quality just before the falls. For those with 4WD, the road makes a twisting ascent to the top of Aztec Peak, the highest point in the Sierra Ancha at 7,694 feet. But I continued hoofing it up the road with the splashy echo of the stream keeping me company to reach the trailhead for Abbey's Way (see Hiking).

As you continue heading south on 288, you'll soon trade dirt for pavement and the tall pines for the tall cacti. As you leave the forest behind and approach the desert basin, spectacular panoramas of Theodore Roosevelt Lake come into view. Those long fingers of blue add a surprising sparkle to the arid landscape. The road winds through mountains adorned with rocky slabs and lanky saguaros. A few swooping curves later, and you're crossing a one-lane bridge over the Salt River. The scenic drive ends, as does Arizona 288 at the junction of Arizona 188. Turn left to reach the mining towns of Miami and Globe.

More Scenic Driving

To truly appreciate the staggering immensity of the Mogollon Rim, you need to spend some time atop its forested roof. Drive Forest Road 300 between Arizona 260 and Arizona 87, 45 miles of well-graded dirt, also known as the Rim Road. This is part of the original wagon road built by

General George Crook to move troops and supplies between military posts in the 1870s as the US Army fought the Apache tribes. For most of the journey, it plays peekaboo with the edge of the Rim, skirting timber, meadows, and a chain of lakes (see Hiking). Often the road lies just a few feet from the cliff. There are plenty of places to pull over. Grab a high ledge, put your back against a tree, and prop your feet up on a cloud. Travel east from Payson for 30 miles, or west from FR 512 (Desert to Tall Pines Scenic Road) for 3 miles to Forest Road 300.

Hiking

WOODS CANYON LAKE LOOP

Perched atop the Mogollon Rim is a collection of lakes formed by damming small canyons. The most popular of these is Woods Canyon Lake with campgrounds, picnic areas, boat rentals, and a small store. Best of all, an easy 5.2-mile trail crosses the earthen dam and traces the water's edge except for one small area where it swings wide to protect a bald eagle nest. Shafts of sunlight stream through the forest canopy, illuminating clumps of ferns and wild roses. Travel east from Payson for 30 miles to Forest Road 300 (Rim Road). Turn left on FR 300 and continue 4 miles to the turnoff for Woods Canyon Lake. (928) 535-7300, www.fs.usda.gov/asnf.

PLEASANT VALLEY VISTA LOOP TRAIL

From the mountain overlook south of Young, a trail dips into the woods and quickly splits. Take either path as it circles a knob of a hill with views of the valley

An easy hiking trail circles Woods Canyon Lake atop the Mogollon Rim, a few miles west of Desert to Tall Pines Scenic Road. Photo by the author.

Near the southern terminus of Desert to Tall Pines, the road crosses a narrow bridge above the Salt River. Photo by the author.

below. A couple of well-positioned benches give you a chance to stop and catch your breath. Since the trail is only 0.7 miles long you probably won't need the break, but it doesn't hurt to take advantage of a peaceful big country panorama.

ABBEY'S WAY #151

Edward Abbey, the late novelist and activist, manned the fire lookout atop Aztec Peak for a few summers in the 1970s. Named in his honor, the trail skirts a large meadow then turns east toward Aztec Peak where it begins climbing through mixed woods in a series of switchbacks. You'll gain 800 feet in elevation in just a couple of miles as you scramble to the peak. Proceed with caution, because the trail can be overgrown in places. During my last visit I cut my hike short when I came upon a bear foraging nearby. The trailhead is located a half-mile past Workman Creek Falls on FR 487, so you may need 4WD to reach it or be willing to walk down the road. The trail rejoins 487 near the top of Aztec Peak. (928) 474-7900, www.fs.usda.gov/tonto.

Where to Eat and Stay

BRUZZI VINEYARD, YOUNG

This small vineyard is one of the only ones in Arizona that focuses on higher elevation hybrid varietals. Along with a tasting room and farm stand, they also serve food Friday through Sunday. In addition to the meat-and-cheese board, they dish up salads, sandwiches, calzones, and homemade pizzas with some intriguing combinations like prosciutto and artichoke, and bacon and jalapeno. 47209 N. Arizona 288, (928) 462-3314, www.bruzzivineyard.com.

PLEASANT VALLEY INN, YOUNG

If you want to linger and enjoy some of the peace and quiet that Young is known for, Pleasant Valley Inn sits in the heart of town. Ten quaint rooms, all slightly different, make a comfortable getaway. Even though you're in the middle of nowhere, it doesn't mean you have to make sacrifices. Each room has a fireplace, DirectTV, refrigerator, microwave, and coffee maker. There's also a restaurant on the property. Arizona 288 and Midway Ave., (928) 462-3593.

When You Go

Pleasant Valley and Young: www.youngaz.com.

Pleasant Valley Museum: 48382 Arizona 288, (928) 462-7847.

CENTRAL DESERTS

A car begins the steep descent down Fish Creek Hill on the Apache Trail Historic Road. Photo by the author.

Apache Trail Historic Road

Overview Traversing the Salt River Valley, this road skirts the Superstition Mountains, twists down Fish Creek Hill, and brushes past a chain of lakes as dramatic scenery unfolds along each and every mile.

Route Numbers Arizona State Highway 88.

Mileage The scenic drive is 41.5 miles (Milepost 201 to Milepost 242.5).

Special Notes This is one of four Historic Roads in the state. Much of the route is unpaved. While suitable for sedans, expect hairpin curves and mountain grades along one portion. Scars may be visible in places from the 2019 Woodbury Fire. The Apache Trail can be combined with the Gila-Pinal Scenic Road to form a loop drive of 120 miles.

If you've ever looked at your knuckles and thought they were too darned pink, you can remedy that with a drive on the Apache Trail. The rangy, historic road in central Arizona exposes a dramatic combination of desert, mountains, and lakes, while the twisting descent down Fish Creek Hill will have even confident drivers clutching the steering wheel in a white-knuckled panic grip.

A winding backcountry drive that delivers stunning scenery and for a few minutes scares the bejeebers out of you—tell me that doesn't sound like a fantastic day.

President Theodore Roosevelt sure thought so. He called the 42-mile road "one of the most spectacular, best-worth-seeing sights in the world." And I'm with Teddy on this one. The Apache Trail proves to be one of the most scenic drives in Arizona and is rich with history as well. It begins in the town of Apache Junction, some 30 miles east of Phoenix.

Native Americans used the route for centuries. The Salados traveled into the Salt River Valley since AD 900. It continued to serve as a corridor for tribes migrating between winter homes in the desert to summer camps in higher elevations.

Officially known as Arizona 88, the Apache Trail angles north from its intersection with US 60 in Apache Junction. The road rambles into a landscape so wild and unexpected it could have been designed by Dr. Seuss after a tequila bender. The Apache Trail travels along the northern flank of the fabled Superstition Mountains, a rowdy wall of jagged peaks and spires.

You'll find a cluster of worthy stops right away, including the Superstition Mountain Museum. The main building is flanked by the Apacheland Barn and Elvis Memorial Chapel, the only structures that survived a fire at nearby Apacheland Movie Ranch. Through the years, dozens of movies and television shows were filmed at Apacheland, including *Gunfight at the O.K. Corral*, *Have Gun, Will Travel*, and *Charro!*, starring Elvis Presley in a non-singing role.

Of course you'll also find authentic equipment like a rare twenty-stamp mill, and lots of intriguing exhibits. The museum is a good place to learn about Jacob Waltz, the German prospector known as the "Dutchman." There are several variations of the tale of the Lost Dutchman Mine, but the main thrust goes like this: during the 1840s, the Peralta family of Mexico operated several mining claims, one of them a rich gold mine deep within the Superstitions. An expedition returning gold ore to Mexico was attacked by Apaches, and all but one of the miners perished.

Jacob Waltz discovered the mine in the 1870s, possibly aided by information from a member of the Peralta family. Waltz worked the claim and allegedly killed anyone who ventured too close. On his deathbed in 1891, Waltz finally described the location of the mine to a neighbor, but she was unable to locate it.

Geologists will state pretty adamantly that the volcanic terrain of the Supes—as they're known locally—make the existence of any gold highly improbable. But that never dampened enthusiasm for the legend. In the ensuing years, hundreds of treasure seekers have searched for the fabled hole. Gruesome murders and strange disappearances followed, cementing the sinister reputations of the Superstition Mountains.

Just up the road is Goldfield Ghost Town. The little burg went bust a few years after gold was discovered in 1892. Nearly a century later it was re-created as a popular tourist destination. Weathered plank buildings, creaky wooden boardwalks, and majestic mountain vistas provide an Old West feel. Arizona's only narrow-gauge train circles the town. Take a short mine tour, watch gunfights, visit a museum, and tour a bordello—although one that no longer receives gentlemen callers.

My favorite stop is just across the road from Goldfield, the Lost Dutchman State Park (see Hiking). Nestled at the base of sheer cliffs, the park features a network of beautiful trails crisscrossing green slopes that often blaze with color in spring. The park is a great place to search for wildflowers in February and March.

Beyond the park, the road curves into a jumble of chaotic hills and tilted ridges before reaching Canyon Lake. The cliff-lined waterway is one of a chain of lakes formed by dams that corral the Salt River. There's a campground here along with a restaurant and cantina. For an up-close look at the soaring cliffs that define the rugged shoreline of Canyon Lake, take a scenic cruise on Dolly Steamboat. The ninety-minute tour explores secluded inner waterways with frequent sightings of desert bighorn sheep, bald eagles, and other wildlife. Enjoy the captain's narration from a comfortable seat in the lower or upper cabins or open-air observation areas. Twilight dinner cruises are another popular outing.

Past Canyon Lake, the Apache Trail rolls through the tiny burg of Tortilla Flat, a former stage stop. Grab a burger or ice cream at this rickety outpost. There's usually a band playing on the patio during winter weekends. This will be your last contact with civilization for a while. The pavement plays out soon after you leave the Flat, but the well-graded dirt is generally no problem for sedans.

A rest area sits atop Fish Creek Hill with views of colorful gorges and jumbled mountains. Even if you go no further, you've had a pretty amazing drive. But the best is yet to come. The road plunges steeply down Fish Creek Hill, dropping 1,500 feet in 3 miles. A seemingly impossible design, the route is one lane with pullouts and curls around the mountain like a stripe on a barber pole. Remember that traffic crawling uphill has the right of way.

Once you reach the bottom of the grade and are just starting to relax, imagine someone springing from behind a boulder, shoving a sawed-off shotgun in your face and demanding your valuables. You're probably a century too late, but scenic Fish Creek Canyon was once the domain of another legendary character, highwayman Hacksaw Tom.

Wearing a flour-sack mask with knife-slit eyeholes, Hacksaw waylaid stagecoaches and teamsters. After collecting his loot, he would go bounding into the rough canyon on foot, leaping from boulder to boulder

---

Travel Note Some historians think Jacob Waltz used nuggets he pilfered from the mine at Goldfield, which lies outside the Superstition Mountains, to represent his mysterious mine.

The Elvis Chapel, once part of the Apacheland Movie Ranch, is now located at the Superstition Mountain Museum. Photo by the author.

and disappearing. He never fired a shot and was never caught or identified.

The rest of the drive is less terrifying. The road rambles alongside Fish Creek, beneath a canopy of cottonwood trees. Saguaros dot the slopes above. Soon you're skirting the shoreline of Apache Lake, with water practically lapping against the shoulder of the road.

As you reach Roosevelt Dam, the pavement resumes, but this is the official end of the Apache Trail. The road was built from 1903 to 1905 to accommodate construction of the masonry dam, which was the tallest in the world when completed. The dam was dedicated in March 1911 by President Theodore Roosevelt, who continued to be most impressed by the journey to get there.

"The Apache Trail combines the grandeur of the Alps, the glory of the Rockies, the magnificence of the Grand Canyon and then adds an indefinable something that none of the others have. To me, it is the most awe-inspiring and most sublimely beautiful panorama nature has ever created," declared Roosevelt.

Roosevelt Lake is the largest man-made lake entirely within Arizona's borders, and is a paradise for anglers and boaters. Turn right onto Arizona 188 to reach Tonto National Monument, showcasing two beautifully preserved Salado cliff dwellings. Built in natural caves on the low flanks of the Superstition Mountains and overlooking Roosevelt Lake, the structures date back more than seven hundred years. The Salado were known for their artistic flair, producing exquisite polychrome pottery and intricately woven textiles. Artifacts found at the site are on display in the visitor center. The Lower Cliff Dwelling is open all year and can be reached by a steep paved path for a 1-mile round trip. The larger Upper Cliff Dwelling is accessible only by guided tours November through April.

If you are returning to Apache Junction and don't want to retrace your route, you can make a loop by continuing southeast on Arizona 188 to Globe, then turning west on US 60, the Gila–Pinal Scenic Road. Along the way you'll enjoy more amazing scenery and worthwhile attractions.

Hiking

TREASURE LOOP TRAIL

Located in Lost Dutchman State Park, the Treasure Loop makes a swooping 2.4-mile climb to the base of sheer cliffs and returns. Starting from either the Cholla or Saguaro day-use areas, the trail gains 500 feet as it brushes past distinctive formations like Green Boulder and the Praying Hands. Connect to other park trails to extend the hike or just enjoy some spectacular views back across the valley. Fee. (480) 982-4485, www.azstateparks.com.

SECOND WATER TRAIL #236

A lovely path slashing across open desert for 3.3 miles. From the First Water Trailhead, set out on the Dutchman's Trail for a few minutes before veering onto Second Water. In these sunbaked hills, it's not surprising that good old H2O receives plenty of attention. Near the halfway point the trail crosses Garden Valley, a level area dense with chain fruit cholla and, following rainy winters, ablaze in wildflowers. From there, you'll make a moderate descent down rocky slopes to the intersection with the Boulder Canyon Trail in a little riparian oasis. About a mile north of Lost Dutchman State Park, turn right on Forest Road 78 and continue 3 miles to First Water Trailhead. (480) 610-3300, www.fs.usda.gov/tonto.

BOULDER CANYON TRAIL #103

Park at Canyon Lake Marina in designated spots for hikers, then cross the road and start climbing a moderately steep hill. When you pause to catch your breath, you'll enjoy some beautiful views of the water below. The trail continues along a high ridge with ever-expanding vistas, including the distinctive hump of Weavers Needle rising in the south and chiseled rock columns closer to hand. The trail eventually drops in and out of La Barge Canyon and then Boulder Canyon. It ends at the Dutchman's Trail at 7.3 miles. (480) 610-3300, www.fs.usda.gov/tonto.

Where to Eat and Stay

SUPERSTITION RESTAURANT & SALOON, TORTILLA FLAT

Among the handful of businesses in Tortilla Flat is the Superstition Restaurant & Saloon, and it looks just like you hope. Plank floors, saddles for bar stools, and walls papered with dollar bills. They serve big burgers, big salads, Mexican grub, and hearty chili in a bread bowl. Save room for prickly pear gelato in the ice cream shop next door. The patio is open during the winter. (480) 984-1776, www.tortillaflataz.com.

ROOSEVELT LAKE MARINA

Enjoy some of the most unique accommodations in Arizona when you stay at the Roosevelt Lake Marina floating motel. The on-the-water unit (with two bedrooms and one bathroom) comes with a kitchen and can sleep six to eight people. Enjoy the soft stillness that settles across the big lake in the evening. This isn't a houseboat; there's no motor, so you won't be able to take it out for a spin. (602) 977-7170, www.rlmaz.com.

When You Go

Superstition Mountain Museum: Fee. 4087 N. Apache Trail, (480) 983-4888, www.superstitionmountainmuseum.org.

Goldfield Ghost Town: (480) 983-0333, www.goldfieldghosttown.com.

Dolly Steamboat: Fee. (480) 827-9144, www.dollysteamboat.com.

Tonto National Monument: Fee. (928) 467-2241, www.nps.gov/tont.

Tilted peaks of the curiously fractured landscape along US 60 dwarf the steel span of Queen Creek Bridge. Photo by the author.

Gila–Pinal Scenic Road

Overview Rising from the desert floor east of Phoenix, the road travels through four biotic communities as it crosses the northern flank of the Pinal Mountains reaching the mining towns of Miami and Globe.

Route Numbers US Highway 60.

Mileage The scenic road is 26 miles (Milepost 214.5 to Milepost 240.5). It's 88 miles from Phoenix to Globe.

Special Notes This highway can be combined to form a loop with the Apache Trail Historic Road and provides access to Copper Corridor Scenic Road West, Copper Corridor Scenic Road East, and Desert to Tall Pines Scenic Road. It overlaps a portion of Historic Arizona US Route 80.

Diversity doesn't begin to describe what this road offers. Attend a Renaissance Festival, hike Silly Mountain, visit the World's Smallest Museum, and drive to the Top-of-the-World. And those aren't even the real highlights, which come in the form of dramatic scenery that transforms every few miles—wildflower-carpeted desert, folded mountains standing on end, ramparts of stone pillars, and canyons shaded with bowed oak trees. Apaches fought for the land and deep veins of silver and copper caused entire towns to spring up almost overnight.

Heading east on US 60 from Apache Junction, the road flows along the southern edge of the Superstition Mountains, the most legend-soaked range in the Southwest. The sheer-sided volcanic remnants are thought by many to shelter the famous Lost Dutchman Mine, brimming with gold. As the story goes, a German immigrant named Jacob Waltz, better known as the Dutchman, discovered an old mine once owned by the Peralta family. He kept it a closely guarded secret until sharing a few cryptic directions on his deathbed. The mine has never been located.

The key to finding the hidden treasure of the Lost Dutchman revolves around Weavers Needle, a sliver of stubborn volcano that has been whittled into a distinctive standalone peak over the eons. Reportedly, the Needle's shadow points the way to the mine at a certain time of day, at a certain time of year. Easy peasy. Just a few miles outside of Apache Junction, you'll pass Peralta Road on the left, which leads to the hiking trail that provides a closer look at Weavers Needle (see Hiking).

Knights, jesters, and wenches take over a corner of the Sonoran Desert just past Peralta Road in February and March. It may seem like an odd juxtaposition, but the sprawling Renaissance Festival has been a tradition since 1987. Located 7 miles east of Apache Junction, the medieval amusement park includes multistage theatres, jousting tournaments, a circus, feast, and marketplace. It's open on weekends.

Following wet winters, wildflowers drown the hillsides along the roadway. You'll see a mix of poppies, lupines, and phacelia for the first several miles. Brittlebush, desert marigolds, and globemallows take center stage as the road climbs through Gonzales Pass. I consider this to be one of the best wildflower drives in the state with peak color usually occurring March through early April.

The official portion of the scenic drive begins at Florence Junction, about 16 miles east of Apache Junction. Arizona 79 heads south from here as US 60 continues northeast, soon entering the Tonto National Forest. Big broad-shouldered Picketpost Mountain looms on the right side of the highway. The 4,375-foot mountain was named for a military camp established at the site to battle the Apaches.

Nestled at the base of Picketpost is

Spring wildflowers are often on display along the Gila-Pinal Scenic Road. Courtesy of Mike Koopsen, Sedona.

Boyce Thompson Arboretum, a shady sanctuary that harbors over 4,000 different types of drought-tolerant plants from cacti to succulents to a forest of hardy trees from arid regions all across the globe. Founded by wealthy mining engineer, Colonel William Boyce Thompson, the arboretum is crisscrossed by easy hiking trails (some wheelchair accessible) that explore a variety of themed gardens and even a small lake.

Past the arboretum, you hit the outskirts of Superior. Keep an eye peeled for the World's Smallest Museum because . . . well, it's really, really small. It may not be the world's smallest anymore (an even tinier museum opened in an elevator shaft in New York City), but they pack an interesting oddball collection of stuff into 134 square feet of space. Exhibits include ore samples from nearby mines, old typewriters, a Beatles concert poster, and the world's largest Apache tear, rounded pebbles of black obsidian. Located on the grounds of Buckboard City Café, the museum is free and open during café hours.

Just up the road, a red caboose serves as a Superior Visitor Center (there's also a more traditional office downtown) and is surrounded by the Superior History Trail, a paved walking path lined with big pieces of rusted mining equipment. Superior, like Miami and Globe further east, began as a mining town when silver and then a vast copper deposit was discovered. But unlike the Dutchman's legendary hole in the ground, Superior is the story of a lost mine that actually did exist and was found again. Best of all, it delivered on all its promise of wealth. (For details of the Silver King Mine's discovery, see Copper Corridor Scenic Road West.)

Past Superior the road begins a steep climb through curiously tilted peaks. It crosses a high bridge surrounded by the fractured and folded rocks of the Pinal Mountains. Snake through 1,217-foot-long Queen Creek Tunnel and when you emerge from the shadowy LED-lit cocoon, it feels like you've entered another world, one ruled by a race of stone giants. Canyon walls bristle with pillars, turrets, and sculpted ridgelines.

There are pullouts to stop and admire this army of stone that appears so animate and full of personality. Scan the crags and ledges, and you'll likely spot spider-sized figures crawling up the vertical faces. This is a popular destination for rock climbers. Just ahead Oak Flat Campground offers sixteen campsites among the boulders and trees. Nearby Devil's Campground only supports five sites but also has a picnic area.

Instead of teetering atop some high summit, the small community of Top-of-the-World is strung across a shady benchland. But don't hold their hyperbolic name against them. Stop and browse in the little hodgepodge antique shops if they're open.

The road drops down Bloody Tanks Wash, named for another massacre of Apaches, this time during the pretense of a peace parley when the white settlers fired from ambush, killing nineteen warriors. The dying Indians crawled over rocks to the creek, their blood staining the water.

Approaching Miami, the road passes a geometrically precise terraced mountain. These are the mine tailings extracted from the big mines that have produced more than two billion pounds of copper. But it's obvious that Miami has seen better days. Too many of the historic buildings downtown stand vacant.

Look closer and you'll find a few businesses still going. Antique shops, galleries, and restaurants are hanging on as Miami finds its way forward. The Bullion Plaza Cultural Center and Museum showcases the surprising diversity of the region where immigrants from all over the world came to work the mines or open businesses. This was once the segregated school for Mexican and Apache children, where kids were swatted for speaking their native tongue. So it's a nice bit of karmic justice that today it celebrates the different cultures that were part of the community with photographs and artifacts, including Mexican, Slavic, and Native American exhibits.

Globe has fared better than Miami. The historic downtown is filled with shops, restaurants, saloons, and a movie theater. Nearby Besh Ba Gowah Archaeological Park and Museum preserves a partially

Travel Note The massive wall of rock overlooking Superior is known as Apache Leap. Legend has it that a band of Apache warriors were cornered atop the high cliff by soldiers of the US Cavalry. Rather than surrender or be killed, seventy-five warriors leaped to their death. The Apache women wept for the dead and their tears turned to black stones. These are now known as Apache tears.

restored ancient pueblo of the Salado people dating back to AD 1225.

Hiking

SILLY MOUNTAIN PARK

What hiker can resist the siren song of a jaunt to Silly Mountain? Once a chewed-up off-roading playground bearing some ugly scars, Silly Mountain has been turned into a lovely park with a network of short family-friendly trails. You can put together a variety of loops across the restored terrain, ranging from easy to moderate with only a couple of brief steep patches, like the 0.2-mile Huff & Puff Trail. Enjoy impressive views of the Supes and the Valley of the Sun. From US 60 near Milepost 200, turn north on S. Silly Mountain Road. www.azsalt.org.

PERALTA TRAIL #102

This heavily trafficked trail provides an iconic introduction to the Superstition Mountain Wilderness. After crossing a wash, it's a steady uphill slog through boulder-strewn desert to the Fremont Saddle, a high ledge overlooking Weavers Needle. Rising almost 1,300 feet from its base, the angled blade of volcanic stone is said to hold the key to the Lost Dutchman treasure. Although the Peralta Trail continues into the wilderness connecting to other routes, most folks use the saddle as their turnaround point for a 4.5-mile round-trip hike. Another option is to hike the additional half-mile on well-worn social paths to the lone pine tree on the ridge east of the needle for even more stunning views. From US 60, turn north on Peralta Road near Milepost 204 and proceed to the trailhead. The unpaved portion is manageable in a sedan. (480) 610-3300, www.fs.usda.gov/tonto.

Travel Note In downtown Globe, the Hanging Tree Memorial marks the spot where two men were strung up from a sycamore in 1882 for a holdup and double murder. An on-site plaque describes the incident: "The culprits had a fair hearing before JP Allen on Wednesday eve. and at 2 am Thursday on a clear night they were hanged. Saloons were closed and it was an orderly lynching."

ROUND MOUNTAIN PARK

Nestled in the hills on the east side of Globe, this park exists almost exclusively for hiking. There are six hiking trails of varying lengths that ramble over the slopes and flow through shallow canyons. Both West Trail (0.8 miles) and East Trail (1 mile) climb to the summit, gaining a bit over 400 feet. Kids will enjoy the short Bull's Eye Rock Loop, leading to a window gouged into a wall of stone with plenty of small arches, grottoes,

A few streets filled with historic buildings comprise downtown Miami. Photo by the author.

and play-sized caves begging for a little exploration. Round Mountain Park is located at the end of South Street off US 60.

Where to Eat and Stay

GUAYO'S EL REY, MIAMI

Since 1938, this family restaurant in Miami has been known for their heaping portions of traditional Sonoran cuisine. The big combination plates allow diners to sample a range of old favorites and new flavors. The mix of flour and corn tortilla chips go well with the homemade salsa. Start things off with the green chili cheese crisp, although it's practically a meal unto itself. 716 Sullivan St., (928) 473-9960.

NURD BERGER CAFÉ, GLOBE

The small funky place feels like a teenage fever dream inside, overflowing with nerdy Star Wars, super hero, and comic book paraphernalia. The force is definitely with the juicy burgers. You'll have several to choose from, including the half-pound Raising Arizona, assembled from statewide ingredients. They also do chicken, fish, and steak sandwiches and have plenty of fresh-baked desserts on hand. Dine inside or on the dog-friendly patio. 420 S. Hill St., (480) 316-0882.

NOFTSGER HILL INN, GLOBE

A former schoolhouse in Globe has been converted into a welcoming bed-and-breakfast with classrooms reimagined as spacious suites decorated with antiques and artwork. The coatrooms have been turned into private bathrooms with claw-foot tubs. Anyone who likes to spread out on vacation will give high marks to these 900-square-foot rooms with views of the rugged Pinal Mountains. 425 North St., (928) 425-2260, www.noftsgerhillinn.com.

Pillars of stone and craggy cliffs greet travelers emerging from Queen Creek Tunnel. Photo by the author.

When You Go

Arizona Renaissance Festival: Fee. 12601 E. US 60, Gold Canyon. (520) 463-2600, arizona.renfestinfo.com.

Boyce Thompson Arboretum: Fee. 37615 E. Aboretum Way, Superior. (520) 689-2723, www.btarboretum.org.

World's Smallest Museum/Buckboard City Café: 1111 W. US 60, Superior. (520) 689-5800.

Superior Chamber of Commerce: The visitor center is at 165 Main St. (and red caboose at the park on US 60). (520) 689-0200, www.superiorarizonachamber.org.

Bullion Plaza Cultural Center and Museum: 150 N. Plaza Circle, Miami. (928) 473-3700, www.bullionplazamuseum.org.

Globe–Miami Chamber of Commerce: Look for the Gila County Historical Museum, adjacent to the visitor center at 1360 N. Broad St. (928) 425-4495, www.globemiamichamber.com.

Copper Corridor Scenic Road West

Overview Exploring the rich mining history of Central Arizona, this road travels through rugged mountains to fertile river valleys.

Route Numbers Arizona State Highway 177.

Mileage The scenic road is 15 miles (Milepost 149 to Milepost 164). It is 32 miles from Superior to Winkelman.

Special Notes This short highway connects with two other scenic roads, Gila–Pinal Scenic Road at its northern terminus and Copper Corridor Scenic Road East at the south end.

Mining towns often look a little worn around the edges because they're married to the boom-bust cycle. Things always seem to be in a state of flux. People move in or people move out. Businesses extend their hours or close up shop. Everything seems to hinge on so many outside factors—fluctuating prices, changing technology, and quality and accessibility of the ore.

One segment of Legends of Superior Trail (LOST) follows the original alignment of US 60 and offers interpretive signage along the way. Photo by the author.

Travel Note Every August, Superior holds a Prickly Pear Festival celebrating the many uses of this hardworking cactus. Its ripe fruit can be turned into syrup, jam, ice cream, salad dressing, and margaritas just to name a few, and it contains antiviral and anti-inflammatory properties.

Sometimes the bust is too devastating to overcome, the mine closes, and the community withers away to nothing. Most crumbling ghost towns scattered across the Arizona landscape were once connected to mining. Sometimes the boom is big enough to sustain a population through the lean times long enough to carve out an entirely new identity. Take Bisbee, Jerome, and Tombstone for example.

Superior hasn't gotten to that point yet. The town is still finding its way forward, but I've been impressed with recent strides. For years it felt like the community in the Pinal Mountains was a mere husk that one strong wind would sweep into the canyons. Suddenly, it's charming again. Nestled at the base of Apache Leap Mountain and filled with historic buildings, Superior features a picturesque downtown on an upswing. Several new businesses have opened, and in 2017 the Chamber of Commerce initiated a program to spruce up once dilapidated properties. New murals, fresh coats of paint, and landscaped parks add a welcoming touch.

From Superior, Arizona 177 heads south past saguaro-dotted slopes and rocky cliffs. The Dripping Springs Mountains run along the east side of the road and display examples of tilted Paleozoic sedimentary rocks. The road soon drops into Walnut Canyon. About 15 miles south of Superior, you'll reach the small community of Kelvin. There's not much to distinguish it, but branching to the right is the

Copper Corridor West offers some nice desert scenery as well as a lesson in Arizona mining history. Photo by the author.

Florence–Kelvin Highway, providing access to a segment of the Arizona National Scenic Trail (see Hiking) as well as making a winding dirt-road drive across open desert to the town of Florence.

Just south of Teapot Mountain, the pastel terraces of the Ray Operations come into sight. But the staggering size of the open-pit mine is not immediately apparent. Carved from mountain flanks, the oddly precise geometric gouge in the landscape begins to dominate as you continue south.

One of the things I find most fascinating about this road is that Arizona 177 traces the arc of Arizona's mining history in the matter of a few miles. It travels from the first primitive holes dug by hand or blasted by dynamite to the technologically sophisticated large-scale extractions of today.

Start with the Silver King Mine that led to the founding of Superior. In the early 1870s, the US Army began construction of a wagon road to connect the small military camp at the base of Picketpost Mountain and the proposed site of Camp Pinal to the east. While working on the road, a soldier named Sullivan discovered a curious outcrop of black rock. He pocketed a sample and later showed it to a local rancher named Mason who identified it as a high-grade specimen of silver. Sullivan wouldn't reveal the location of his discovery, intending to return and stake a claim. After mustering out of the army he returned but was unable to find his black rock again. He drifted west to California seeking other fortune.

Mason never forgot about the silver and eventually organized a party to search for it near the wagon road. While prospecting the men were attacked by Apaches. The brief exchange of gunfire sent a pack mule running. When the men went to fetch the animal they found it standing atop an outcrop of black rock. Claims were immediately filed on the Silver King Mine. It would go on to be the richest silver mine in Arizona history.

As for Sullivan, he never struck it rich in California. Years later he showed up destitute at the Silver King. But instead of getting the bum's rush by the new owners, he was given a job and a small pension for his initial discovery—a surprisingly fair shake for the times.

Although the Silver King would begin to falter in the late 1880s, its initial success led to the founding of the nearby Silver Queen Mine, which in turn led to the discovery of vast deposits of copper.

The Ray Mining District was also organized in 1880 during the search for silver. The work moved in fits and starts according to the whims of the market. Mine ownership changed hands several times. Then in 1955, underground workings were discontinued at the Ray and its open-pit operation began.

The road skirts the edge of the gaping maw that is now the Ray, a lunar-like canyon. There's a designated pullout with an overlook if you want to try to grasp the scale of the thing. Yes, those are very large trucks crawling like a line of ants along different terraces. Today, the Ray is operated by ASARCO and consists of an open-pit mine that produces 250,000 tons per day, with projected ore reserves lasting until 2044.

The communities of Ray, Sonora, and Barcelona were swallowed by the mine, which led to the building of Kearny in the late 1950s to relocate miners and their families. The railroad tracks you see are part of the Copper Basin Railway, used to transport ore from the mine to the processing facilities at Hayden. Besides the smelter, the business district is a little thin throughout Hayden. The last few miles of 177 run alongside the Gila River.

The Tortilla Mountains lie beyond the Gila as the basin widens. Arizona 177 ends in the town of Winkelman at Arizona 77 (Copper Corridor Scenic Road East). This is also where the San Pedro River joins the Gila.

Travel Note The San Pedro River is the last major, free-flowing undammed river in the Southwest.

Not as reliant on the mines as some of the neighboring communities, Winkelman remains a bit livelier. It claims to be the smallest incorporated town in Arizona. Winkelman Flats Public Park sits on the banks of the Gila River and offers RV camping with utility hookups, dry camping areas, a playground for children, picnic areas, fishing, canoeing, and tubing.

To continue to Tucson (67 miles), turn right on Arizona 77. Travelers heading to Globe (36.5 miles) should turn left on Arizona 77.

Hiking

LEGENDS OF SUPERIOR TRAIL (LOST)

Starting from downtown Superior at the corner of Main and Magma, this wide interpretive path meanders east along Queen Creek as it follows the original alignment of US 60. Hikers are treated to views of high canyon walls, a unique perspective of the steel-arch bridge that spans the canyon, and informational signage. The trail climbs through the old highway tunnel. Return the way you came for a 4-mile round trip. The western segment of LOST stretches for 6 miles past the ghost town of Pinal City and connects to the Arizona Trail. (520) 689-0200, www.superiorarizonachamber.org.

PICKETPOST MOUNTAIN

Only consider making the climb to the top of this prominent peak rising west of

Superior if you're fit and looking for a challenge. This is more scramble than hike, gaining nearly 2,000 feet in 2 miles. So it's tough going anyway, but compounding that is the sketchy condition of the trail, which means it's easy to stray. Be prepared to bushwhack through desert scrub. The payoff is a delicious 360-degree view of the rough heart of Central Arizona. Surprisingly, at the summit you'll find a red mailbox. It holds the trail register and the occasional gift left by other hikers. It's not on any mail-carrier's route, so don't leave your cousin's birthday card behind with the flag up and expect it to be delivered. The trail is not suitable for dogs, kids, or sane people. Look for the signed turnoff for the trailhead south of US 60 near Milepost 221.

GILA RIVER CANYONS PASSAGE 16

The key to this hike is simply forcing yourself to stop. It is a compelling segment of the Arizona Trail that will pull you into thrilling and isolated country. Backpackers are rewarded with views of plunging canyons, striking rock formations, and a wild sense of seclusion. Day hikers will experience a walk along the river. This was the last segment of the Arizona Trail to be completed and a small survey post commemorates that fact 2 miles from the trailhead. Enjoy the riparian corridor and surrounding desert—just don't venture too far. Hike as long as you're comfortable, have a riverside snack, and return the way you came. The full passage is 26 miles. Drive south on the Florence–Kelvin Highway for 1.2 miles and cross the Kelvin Bridge. Passage begins at south end of the old bridge. (602) 252-4794, www.aztrail.org.

Where to Eat and Stay

JADE GRILL, SUPERIOR

This intimate little place is a roadside gem serving a surprisingly diverse range of items from Chinese pork ribs to Korean beef wraps to Thai grilled salad. The owner was a highly successful food writer and editor in New York before returning to her hometown of Superior to give something back. Her passion for barbecue is obvious in the flavorful slow-smoked meats, and she's an artist with the spices and seasonings. 639 W. US 60, (520) 689-2885, www.jadegrillbbq.com.

MARIA'S RESTAURANT, HAYDEN

For tourists, there are not a lot of compelling reasons to stop in Hayden, which is a pretty basic mining town. But if you're feeling peckish and could go for some Mexican food, Maria's Restaurant is popular with the locals. The chorizo and eggs is always a good way to start a day, and the prices are reasonable. 607 W. Arizona 177, (520) 356-6807.

DREAM MANOR INN, GLOBE

This boutique resort perches atop a hill north of Globe and affords guests some sweeping views of the Pinal Mountains and surrounding country. The luscious peaceful property is modeled after a Tuscan village, featuring regular rooms and villas spread across the lovely grounds amid waterfalls, fountains, and terraced gardens. There's also a pool and four-story observation tower on site where you can watch for wildlife or marvel at the sunset. 1 Dream Manor Rd., (928) 425-2754, www.dreammanorinn.com.

When You Go

Superior Chamber of Commerce: The visitor center is at 165 Main St. (and red caboose at the park on US 60). (520) 689-0200, www.superiorarizonachamber.org.

Copper Corridor Scenic Road East

Overview While mining history is very much a part of this drive, the dynamic scenery becomes the focus as the road rises from desert floor north of Oracle through the Gila River gorge of ancient folded limestone walls and over a mountain range, ending in the town of Globe.

Route Numbers Arizona State Highway 77.

Mileage The scenic drive is 38 miles (Milepost 124 to Milepost 162). It is 79 miles from Oracle Junction to Globe.

Special Notes This road connects to Copper Corridor Scenic Road West and provides access to Gila-Pinal Scenic Road. It overlaps a portion of Historic Arizona US Route 80.

There's a wild quality to this road that always sneaks up on me. It starts amid desert hills, passes through a couple of small towns, and shows evidence of the mining past. All that is sort of expected. But along the way you chase two flowing rivers and climb through a dramatic canyon of faulted stone and across a high lonely pass with vistas of mountains that go rambling off in all directions.

Starting from the south, Oracle Junction is located about 24 miles north of Tucson. This is where Arizona 79 and Arizona 77 split. Arizona 79, also known as the Pinal Pioneer Parkway, tracks northwest to the town of Florence. It crosses a high desert plain and flashes plenty of blooms during spring wildflower season.

For this journey, follow Arizona 77 as it heads east with views of the Santa Catalina Mountains. You'll soon spot the turnoff for Biosphere 2. It makes an intriguing stop. Housing seven model ecosystems, the giant laboratory is operated by the University of Arizona and also offers tours. Strange as it seems in the middle of the Sonoran Desert, visitors can experience a tropical rainforest and even smell an ocean complete with coral reef.

Just beyond Biosphere 2, the road edges past but doesn't go through Oracle. You'll have to make the quick turnoff to see the little burg spread across the desert scrub. And I always like to stop. There's a sweet small-town feel to Oracle. You'll find a few restaurants, galleries, guest ranches, a simple museum, and the centerpiece attraction, Oracle State Park. The former ranch features a lovely yet surprising Mediterranean- and Moorish-style home built by the Kannally family between 1929 and 1933. It's certainly not your typical ranch house. Instead it's filled with original furnishings, artwork, and amazing architectural details. Over 15 miles of hiking and biking trails surround the historic home, including a segment of the Arizona National Scenic Trail.

Leaving the park behind, the road descends through open desert with the Galiuro Mountains rising in the east. Entering the small town of Mammoth, you cross the San Pedro River. The Mammoth Miners Memorial honors the men who died working the local mines. The memorial features mining equipment, ore buckets, and a sculpture by Jerry Parra of life-size metal skeletons still toiling away. Look for the memorial on the west side of Arizona 77 near Milepost 114.

After Mammoth, the road swings north following the course of the San Pedro River as it flows toward its meeting with the Gila River. Floodplain farming can be seen

Travel Note Albert Weldon staked the first mining claim in the area in the late 1870s. He named it Oracle, after the name of the clipper ship that carried him from New Brunswick, Canada, around Cape Horn to California.

Pull over to enjoy expansive views from El Capitan Pass. Photo by the author.

along this stretch that's also punctuated with groves of towering saguaro cactus.

The official portion of the scenic road commences upon crossing Aravaipa Creek. The little waterway may not look like much here, but never bet against the sly power of water. In this case it's responsible for carving one of Arizona's most spectacular canyons. The signed road turning right leads to the western end of Aravaipa Canyon, an 11-mile gash along the northern edge of the Galiuro Mountains. But don't go rushing off to explore this oasis just yet. The Bureau of Land Management manages the nearly 20,000-acre wilderness area, and, to protect the fragile environment, permits are required to camp or hike in the canyon (see Hiking).

It's 10 miles to the town of Winkelman where the sight of the smelter stacks of Hayden and a slag pile bring you back to reality. But that's only temporary. There are a couple of different junctions that define Winkelman. This is the confluence of the San Pedro and Gila Rivers, and the southern terminus of Arizona 177 (Copper Corridor Scenic Road West) is here. Winkelman will also be the last services available until you reach Globe. Things are about to take a turn toward the wild side as you continue pushing northeast on Arizona 77.

Almost immediately you begin climbing through a slashing gorge of the Gila River. Landscape that had been open and spread out closes in around you. This is a deep narrow defile with walls of folded limestone. The road curves match the twisting bends of the Gila. This is the last good time for the Gila River, flowing out of the mountains from the Coolidge Dam. Once the river reaches the flatlands, everyone sticks in a straw. For much of the rest of the way as it joins the Colorado River, the Gila is just a wide sandy bed with intermittent pools.

There are a few wide shoulders where you can pull off and enjoy the river sounds and the craggy white cliffs. If you want more than just a glimpse of the water, stop at the Shores Recreation Site near Milepost 141. The dirt road branches to the east and leads through thick brush and trees to the Gila. You won't find many amenities, just a chance to hang out with a desert river while it's still reasonably fat and sassy. Tubing, kayaking, and canoeing are permitted. Primitive campsites are available and include fire rings and vault toilets. Because of the narrow roads and tight turns, it's not suitable for anything larger than a small pickup camper.

The road proceeds along the edge of the Dripping Springs Mountains, winding through the river valley for a bit before turning away from the water and climbing into the Mescal Mountains. This is a furious clutter of white cliffs and angled ridges. Complex fault fissure systems and tilted fault blocks are characteristic of both the Mescals and the Dripping Springs range, giving this stretch of 77 the feel of some exotic but vaguely familiar planet.

Vegetation changes as you continue to curve and climb until reaching El Capitan Pass (4,983 feet). Pull over to enjoy views of assorted mountain ranges spread across the landscape. There are a couple of shaded picnic tables here and a faded historic plaque, commemorating the pass's significance during the Mexican-American War. Guided by Kit Carson, General Stephen Kearny and his Army of the West used the pass in 1846 to avoid the treacherous canyon of the Gila River. After securing Santa Fe and establishing a New Mexico Territory, Kearny and a portion of his men made the arduous mount-killing journey across the Sonoran Desert to lead the fight against Mexican forces in California.

Travel Note Before the Gadsden Purchase in 1853, the Gila River was the US-Mexico Boundary.

From the high perch the road descends quickly through scrubby hills, losing 1,400 feet of elevation as it joins US 60 on the edge of Globe.

More Scenic Driving

In Globe, Arizona 77 and US 60 overlap and continue northeast. The road makes a twisting climb through the Salt River Canyon—often called a mini–Grand Canyon. Expect cliff-hugging curves and hairpin turns and plenty of visual drama. Although there are pullouts and passing lanes, this is not a divided highway so traffic can get a little slow and snarly at times. It's 87 miles from Globe to Show Low, where you'll climb out of the canyon to the forests atop the Mogollon Rim and a horizon of White Mountain peaks. Be prepared for very different weather conditions from one end of the drive to the other.

Hiking

GRANITE OVERLOOK LOOP

Several trails ramble across Oracle State Park in the foothills of the Santa Catalina Mountains. Granite Overlook Loop (1.6 miles) introduces hikers to some of the most enticing scenery as it weaves among slopes crowned with oak trees and boulder piles. Take the moderate trail counterclockwise as it climbs to the highest point in the park, where you'll admire the gleaming white walls of the Kannally Ranch House rising from the desert scrub. Fee. (520) 896-2425, www.azstateparks.com.

ARAVAIPA CANYON WILDERNESS

Managed by the Bureau of Land Management, the wilderness includes the main canyon, the surrounding tablelands, and nine side canyons. Colorful 1,000-foot canyon walls soar overhead sheltering a world that seems far removed from everything. Lining the banks of perennial Aravaipa Creek is a riparian forest of cottonwood, willow, walnut, alder, and sycamore trees. Permits are required to enter—and those are limited to fifty people per day. There are no trails or designated campsites. Most of the time you'll be wading in the stream. Move through gently. Leave no trace. Best time to visit is spring and fall. Permits are available up to thirteen weeks in advance and get snapped up quickly. Fee. (928) 348-4400, recreation.gov.

OLD DOMINION HISTORIC MINE PARK

This Globe park provides a detailed overview of the mining heritage of the region. Open from 1880 to 1931, the Old Dominion produced over 765 million pounds of copper. During reclamation of the site, vegetation was restored and improvements made.

The mining town of Globe is also known for a bounty of good Mexican restaurants and numerous antique and specialty shops. Photo by the author.

A network of trails weaves among old buildings, headframe, equipment, artifacts, and helpful signage. Open from dawn to dusk, the park is free. The main entrance is on Murphy Street (behind DeMarco's Italian Restaurant), just off US 60. (928) 425-7385.

Where to Eat and Stay

DRIFT INN SALOON, GLOBE

The high ceilings of pressed tin, wooden floors, and big murals all conspire to transport you to a different era. Built in 1902, the Drift, as it is affectionately known, retains plenty of historic charm. The menu includes finger food like wings, jalapeno bottle caps, fried pickles, and sandwiches—but the brawny burgers cooked on the flattop are the stars. Two pool tables, shuffleboard, and nightly events keep the locals drifting in. 636 N. Broad St., (928) 425-9573.

ORACLE PATIO CAFÉ AND MARKET, ORACLE

Hang out at Oracle Patio Café and Market for a morning, and you're likely to meet nearly every resident in town. They come for the expansive breakfast menu or an early lunch with fresh salads, sandwiches, and homemade soups. Or maybe they come to do a little grocery shopping, picking up fresh-baked goods, local produce, and meats. Dine inside amid brightly painted murals or outside on the shady patio. 270 American, Ave., (520) 896-7615, www.oraclepatiocafe.com.

CHERRY VALLEY RANCH BED & BREAKFAST, ORACLE

Located right across the road from Oracle State Park, Cherry Valley Ranch Bed & Breakfast sits on one hundred acres of hilly oak woodlands. Accommodations include two guest bedrooms in the main house and two private cottages. Each bedroom has a fireplace and private bath featuring hand-painted tile. Breakfast is served in the dining room overlooking the valley. 2505 E. Mt. Lemmon Rd., (520) 896-9639, www.cherryvalleyranch.com.

CHRYSOCOLLA INN, GLOBE

An old boardinghouse slated for the wrecking ball was saved, beautifully restored and converted to an inviting bed-and-breakfast. Located just a block from Globe's historic downtown, the graceful building is full of architectural details. The six rooms include comfortable vintage furniture. Plus, there are porches, patios, and verandas everywhere you turn, providing a key component for an ultra-restful getaway. 246 E. Oak St., (928) 961-0970, www.chrysocollainn.com.

When You Go

Visit Oracle: 1470 W American Ave., (520) 896-3300, www.visitoracle.org.

Globe–Miami Chamber of Commerce: Look for the Gila County Historical Museum, adjacent to the visitor center at 1360 N. Broad St., (928) 425-4495, www.globemiamichamber.com.

Biosphere 2: Fee. 32540 S. Biosphere Rd. (520) 621-4800, www.biosphere2.org.

Joshua Forest Scenic Road

Overview Traveling between Wickenburg and Wikieup, this is where the Sonoran Desert and Mojave Desert overlap, where stately saguaros rise amid clusters of gangly Joshua trees, and canyons and cliffs define the landscape.

Route Numbers US Highway 93.

Mileage The scenic road is 53.5 miles (Milepost 126.5 to Milepost 180).

Special Notes This road may not be long for this world. The planned corridor for Interstate 11 will connect Phoenix and Las Vegas and—when complete—will likely submerge most of the current scenic road.

I will miss this highway when it's gone—if it does perish. After all, there are no guarantees in the world of infrastructure upgrades. While I certainly understand the need for efficient high-speed interstates, the planned I-11 seems a bit superfluous. It's not like Phoenicians have to endure a winding country road to get their fix of Elvis tribute artists and shrimp cocktails. Much of 93 is a divided four-lane highway allowing travelers to boom across the desert at 65 mph in a long straight shot. Still, I suppose no one wants to be late to the buffet tables. Viva Las Vegas, baby!

The scenic road begins just north of Wickenburg, but don't be in such a hurry to get started. Spend a little time and you'll learn the value of moseying. Downtown Wickenburg is a step back into the past,

Travel Note The Hassayampa River flows mostly underground. Legend has it that anyone who drinks its water will never tell the truth again. Maybe. Since I've drunk from the Hassayampa, I could be making the whole thing up.

Unkempt and shaggy, Joshua trees stand guard in the deserts of western Arizona. Photo by the author.

where century-old buildings line the streets and life moves at a more relaxed pace.

The town was founded in 1863 when Prussian-born Henry Wickenburg discovered a ledge of quartz seamed with gold in the mountains above the Hassayampa River. The Vulture Mine operated until 1942, one of Arizona's most productive gold mines.

Take a walking tour of downtown (an informative guide is available at the visitor center). To go along with the historic buildings are streetscape bronze sculptures of Old West characters. And a few bronze critters, too. Don't jump if you see a Gila monster or tarantula on the sidewalk. They finally had to post a sign next to the rattlesnake because too many folks were freaking out.

Be sure to visit Desert Caballeros Western Museum, where cowboy life and art are well represented with works by Albert Bierstadt, Frederic Remington, Charles Russell, and other heavyweights. Plenty of Western memorabilia accompanies the art, as well as historical dioramas and Native American artifacts.

When you are back on US 93, you'll angle northwest across open country. In just a few miles you'll spot the first Joshua trees rising above the creosote thickets. Boundaries blur and habitats collide here at the confluence of the Sonoran Desert and Mojave Desert.

Joshua trees are a tall unruly swirl of trunk and branches covered with dagger-like leaves. Despite their stabby appearance they are not cactus, nor are they trees. They are a large yucca (*yucca brevifolia*) and a member of the lily family—although once you ponder the many graceful types of lilies, it becomes obvious Joshuas are the black sheep of that clan.

Mormon settlers named the unkempt plants, somehow seeing in them the spirit of biblical leader Joshua with arms upraised in supplication. Stare at a Joshua tree long enough, and you can see all sorts of things. Each tree is part majestic, part mournful, a frenzied dervish of twisted branches. When they are grouped together I feel like I'm studying a frozen image of a raging dance marathon.

The Joshua tree is the signature plant of the Mojave Desert, just as the saguaro cactus is for the Sonoran. This stretch of road is one of the few places where the two icons stand side by side, taking the measure of each other. But for several miles, it's all about the Joshua trees. They gather in rowdy clusters with branches flailing in all directions. It's rare to find such exuberance in the desert.

I'm always surprised when I first notice a lone saguaro among the Joshua trees, standing straight and dignified—looking very much like a designated driver at a party that is beginning to spiral out of control.

The terrain turns hillier, and more saguaros spread along the slopes. By the time the road crosses the Santa Maria River and begins climbing, the Joshua trees have dispersed. It's a long steady climb into rocky hills that are doused in wildflowers during the spring. Jumbles of oddly stacked boulders crown the hills. Here in this eerie, lonely place you should stop at Nothing.

Sadly, while there never was much of anything to Nothing, today it's a mere husk, a tiny ghost town. At one time the community of Nothing included a gas station, garage, a store, a population of four, and, of course, the unusual name that brought it a measure of fame among seasoned road warriors.

I can remember the time when Nothing bustled. Well, bustled as much as a town of four residents ever does. But at least it was open for business. You could pull off the highway, gas up your ride, and buy a cold soft drink. Sometimes that was just enough, that quiet moment deep in the Arizona outback, standing there on the edge of dusk with a lurid light washing over the mountains. I'm sorry those days are gone.

Burro Creek offers a secretive oasis along the Joshua Forest Scenic Road. Photo by the author.

The fields of granite boulders are soon replaced by ragged volcanic cliffs. As you approach Burro Creek Canyon, be alert for the turnoff to the left. It's a mile-long paved road that leads down to an unexpected oasis. Burro Creek flows gently along the base of sweeping cliffs. That permanent water source creates a soothing corridor of greenery, a soft carpet of grass and flowers growing on spongy stream banks, surrounded by shrubs and trees and cattails rising from the water. Such an inviting sliver of wetness in this desert basin attracts plenty of wildlife. The Bureau of Land Management operates a campground overlooking the stream, a hidden gem that includes picnic facilities, an interpretive cactus garden, and walking paths down to the creek.

The scenic road ends in Wikieup, nestled in the Big Sandy Valley and flanked by the Aquarius Mountains to the east and the Hualapai Mountains to the west. A handful of businesses are strung along the road through Wikieup, including a trading post, gas stations, and eateries.

The most unexpected sight is a long white rocket poised for launch, with Snoopy and his posse riding it bronc-style. It's Peanuts meets Dr. Strangelove. Now that's an animated movie I'd check out. Snoopy is atop the rocket along with a mini-Snoopy and his mustachioed brother Spike. Loyal sidekick Woodstock perches on the nose cone. Woodstock is Doc Holliday to Snoopy's Wyatt Earp—and if that's not the first time small, feathered Woodstock has been compared to an Old West gunslinger, I'll be sorely disappointed. As roadside attractions go, this one ranks high on the weirdness meter.

US 93 joins I-40 about 20 miles east of Kingman. It continues into town and then branches north again pointed toward Hoover Dam and Las Vegas beyond. At least until I-11 rings down the final curtain.

Hiking

BOX CANYON

Just north of Wickenburg, this short hike drops down to a scenic stretch of the Hassayampa River cradled by low-rising cliffs. And yes, there's usually water flowing. From the parking area it's an easy walk downstream through deep sand sliced by a thin ribbon of water. After a half-mile, you reach a clutch of large tamarisk trees on a sandy beach. Here the cliff walls buckle inward and a short box canyon is formed. Don't expect anything too dramatic. It's a walk-in closet of a canyon but very picturesque. When you return, if you head upstream about a half-mile past your vehicle you'll reach the Narrows. Here the cliffs close in framing the river with walls only 20 feet apart. From US 93 turn east on Scenic Loop Road (Milepost 195). Travel 7 miles on this unpaved road suitable for sedans. Turn right where a small BLM sign says "No Dumping." Go 0.1 miles and park.

BADGER TRAIL

A network of trails carve up the desert around Kingman. I hope they all survive the onslaught of I-11. The Badger Trail should be safe as it winds its way up the southern slopes of the Cerbat Mountains. A bristly array of yucca, cholla, ocotillo, and beavertail cactus lines the path along with clustered boulders adding visual interest. Even though the trail gains almost 1,100 feet in 3.2 miles it's never strenuous, rising in a series of mild switchbacks. Trail markers appear every half-mile to chart your progress. Badger Trail ends atop a high saddle at the junction with the Castle Rock Trail, a 0.6 mile level path that swoops across a ridgeline to reach a dark basalt formation. Enjoy vistas of Kingman and desert basins along the way. Trailhead is north of Kingman off US 93, just past the Arizona

68 junction. (866) 427-7866, www.gokingman.com.

DOLAN SPRINGS TRAILS

If you want to hike among Joshua trees, you'll need to continue driving north on 93. Look for the turnoff for Dolan Springs (Pearce Ferry Road), 28 miles north of Kingman. Turn east and continue for 7 miles to the small town of Dolan Springs. A group of dedicated volunteers has carved a 6-mile network of interconnected trails out of the high desert at the base of Mt. Mitten. Three different trailheads provide easy access to well-engineered and mostly level paths. Even though you're close to town a sense of solitude pervades as the trails weave among dense groves of Joshua trees. It's a great chance to study these curious plants up close. Some of the most impressive specimens can be found on the T & C and Cholla loops. Trailheads are on Thirteenth, Fourteenth and Fifteenth Street. www.dolanspringstrails.com.

Where to Eat and Stay

LUCHIA'S RESTAURANT & GIFTS, WIKIEUP

Any place where you can eat pie among the peacocks is worth a stop. Especially if it's a slice of black walnut cream, the house specialty of Luchia's. An array of colorful signs out front pull you off the road. There's a surprisingly high-end collection of Indian art and jewelry inside and a dining room serving breakfast and lunch. But it's hard to resist the shady veranda out back, an oasis filled with palm trees, a cactus garden, koi pond, and free-roaming peacocks. The menu includes several Mexican specialties to go along with sandwiches and salads. They make several pies each day, including the popular black walnut cream. 15797 US 93, (928) 765-2229.

MATTINA'S RISTORANTE ITALIANO, KINGMAN

Start with a cozy century-old house and fill it with the sensual aromas of sauces bubbling on the stove and sausage sizzling in the pan, and you've got the perfect setting for a meal. Or the setting for a Martin Scorsese movie. Located in downtown Kingman, Mattina's is known for their authentic Italian cuisine. Try the Sinatra Stuffed Sole, two pieces of tender fish filled with crab meat and scallops, beneath a lemon caper cream sauce. Mattina's is open for dinner only. 318 E. Oak St., (928) 753-7504, www.mattinasristorante.com.

RIO TIERRA CASITAS, WICKENBURG

Nestled on the banks of the Hassayampa River, three airy casitas will transport you to different worlds. Visit Old Mexico, relax in a cowboy bunkhouse, or relive past road trips in a charming mid-century bungalow. It just depends on which of the little guesthouses you choose, each with a full kitchen. In any case you'll love the attention to detail, the artistic furnishings, line-dried linens, and the shady peaceful setting. Get a taste of the delicious breakfast, and you won't want to leave. 28507 US 60, (928) 684-3037, www.riotierracasitas.com.

When You Go

Wickenburg Chamber of Commerce: 216 N. Frontier St., (928) 684-5479, www.wickenburgchamber.com.

Desert Caballeros Western Museum: Fee. 21 N. Frontier St., (928) 684-2272, www.westernmuseum.org.

Burro Creek Recreation Site: BLM Kingman Office, (928) 718-3700.

Kingman Visitor Center: 120 W. Andy Devine Ave., (866) 427-7866, www.gokingman.com.

SOUTHERN ARIZONA

Sky Island Parkway National Scenic Byway

Overview A winding National Forest byway that climbs from the Sonoran Desert on the edge of Tucson to cool forests atop the Santa Catalina Mountains. It gains over 6,000 feet of elevation as it ascends to the top of Mount Lemmon.

Route Numbers General Hitchcock Highway, Catalina Highway, and Mount Lemmon Road.

Mileage The scenic road is 27.2 miles (Milepost 0 to Milepost 25, Milepost 25 to Milepost 25.8, and Milepost 25 to Milepost 26.4).

Special Notes Traffic can be heavy on summer weekends when it is often regulated to avoid overuse. Large motor homes, buses, and trailers over 22 feet may have trouble negotiating steep grades and sharp turns. There are very few places to turn around for big vehicles. The road is open year-round, but winter weather may cause restrictions.

This is the drive that epitomizes Arizona. It's often been said that you can ski and swim in the same day in Arizona, and this is the road that proves it.

Starting from the desert floor in Tucson, this twisting mountain road whisks you to the forested heights of the Santa Catalina Mountains and the snowy slopes of Mount Lemmon, where you'll find the southernmost ski resort in the United States. After you get in a few runs, head back down the hill where you can be swimming in the afternoon. Temperatures near the top can be 30 degrees cooler than the lower desert. In Arizona, we organize our seasons by elevation. It's a good system because you always know where to find the one that you want.

A climber scales a prominent formation high on the slopes of Tucson's Mount Lemmon. Courtesy of Rick Mortensen, Cincinnati.

The road passes through five different life zones, the biological equivalent of traveling from Mexico to Canada, except the journey is all smooshed together in a tidy 27 miles. Naturally, a road filled with this many wonders comes with plenty of names. Besides its formal designation as the Sky Island Parkway, it's commonly referred to as the Catalina Highway. Officially, it's the General Hitchcock Highway, named for the former postmaster general who spearheaded the creation of the road. Prisoners provided the bulk of the labor over a seventeen-year period, from 1933 to 1950.

The Santa Catalina Mountains—rising ramparts of rocky peaks and fierce summits—form the northern border of Tucson. These are among the distinctive "sky islands" of Southern Arizona, isolated mountain ranges surrounded by a sea of desert. The Catalina Highway angles northeast off Tanque Verde Road through Tucson neighborhoods. Passing the forest service boundary, it begins a winding climb toward the high country.

This is one scenic road that drivers get to enjoy with relative ease due to numerous pullouts and overlooks. The first one pops up at just over 2 miles, the Babad Do'ag Vista—Tohono O'odham for "frog mountain." Tucson sprawls below, already feeling far removed.

Saguaros continue to chase you up the

Travel Note Four mountain ranges encircle Tucson. In addition to the Santa Catalinas, the Rincon Mountains rise in the east, the Santa Rita Mountains lie to the south, and the Tucson Mountains anchor the western edge.

---

slope but are soon left behind, gasping for air. The landscape transitions into semidesert grasslands and oak woodlands above 4,000 feet. Before long the brushy chaparral gives way to tall pine and cypress trees and eventually forests of fir, spruce, and aspen as the road continues to climb almost to the summit of Mount Lemmon at 9,157 feet.

Panoramas from the overlooks offer constantly changing perspectives as the road crosses canyons and twists around mountainsides. While most people come to admire the big timber practically a pine cone's throw from the desert, it's the rocks that fascinate me. The Santa Catalinas snarl with rough granite teeth. Pillars, hoodoos, and spires are mingled with jumbled boulder stacks and sheer cliff faces.

I love the coarse texture of the stones juxtaposed against soft forest. The curious shapes and upright posture adds animation to the slopes, an element of craggy drama. It becomes most pronounced near Windy Point, 14 miles from the beginning of the drive and the preeminent overlook.

This rocky plateau juts from the mountain exposing the entire basin below. Views are simply breathtaking. Windy Point sits among some of the best rock climbing in these mountains, so you'll often spot folks clinging to high stone walls or scrambling up standalone towers. And since Windy Point weddings are a popular Tucson tradition, don't be surprised to run into people who are way overdressed for the outdoors. A large parking area, pedestrian crossing, and restrooms help accommodate the steady stream of visitors.

The road continues climbing, soon passing the turnoff to Rose Canyon Lake. The trout-stocked lake sits amid ponderosa pines at 7,200 feet. It's flanked by a campground and picnic area. The seven-acre lake is managed by a concessionaire, so there is a fee for day use and camping.

Travel Note Mount Lemmon is named for Sara Lemmon, a botanist and the first white woman to ascend the peak in 1881.

A couple of miles further on is the Palisades Visitor Center where you can gather information and maps for any hikes you might have planned. Trails branch off from many of the overlooks and pullouts along the Sky Island Parkway.

Recreation opportunities abound as the road slices through cool forest for the last 8 miles past the visitor center. Several picnic areas and a few campgrounds are tucked among the trees. The road continues on to Summerhaven, an idyllic little village. This is where you'll find food, lodging, a general store, and cookies the size of manhole covers from the Cookie Cabin.

When the Aspen Fire scorched the mountaintops in 2003, it destroyed much of Summerhaven. But most businesses and cabins were quickly rebuilt. No one wanted to let go of this little piece of paradise. Burn scars are occasionally visible in the woods but they become less prominent each passing year as the healing continues. Yet let them serve as reminders to always exercise caution in this fragile environment.

The road continues past the village for another mile, ending at the Marshall Gulch Picnic Area along Sabino Creek. This also serves as trailhead for some popular hikes.

Just before reaching Summerhaven, Ski Run Road branches off to the right. This takes you to Ski Valley. During warmer months, they operate the chairlift as a scenic ride up the slopes. The last stretch of highway, now a twisting gravel road, makes its way to the summit trailheads. At the top of Mount Lemmon is a working observatory. The Mt. Lemmon Sky Center is only open to the public during specific events.

While atop the mountain take some time to enjoy the cool temperatures and pine-scented air. Then appreciate the fact that you didn't have to drive all the way to Canada to find it.

Hiking

ASPEN LOOP

This extremely popular 4-mile loop is formed by the Marshall Gulch Trail #3 and a section of Aspen Trail #93. The trailhead is at the very end of Sky Island Parkway, beyond Summerhaven. Marshall Gulch plunges right into deep forest and follows the thread of a slender creek. Thin though it may be, the music of falling water enhances any woodland outing. The trail scrambles out of the gulch as it reaches Marshall Saddle and a five-way trail junction. Hang a left on Aspen. Soon you'll pass a cluster of big boulders, a perfect viewing platform known as Lunch Ledge. Most of this section ambles downhill and, of course, passes through some lovely aspen groves before returning you to the trailhead in the Marshall Gulch Picnic Area.

MEADOW LOOP

Most mountain hikes are going to involve sharp ups or downs depending on where you start. That's what makes this gentle meander such a pleasure. Starting from the summit trailhead at the end of Ski Run Road, set out on the Mount Lemmon Trail #5. It ambles off behind the fenced electrical station, crosses a dirt road, and reaches the junction with the Meadow Trail #5A. Take this fork as the Meadow Trail curves past the observatory and then strikes out along a ridgeline into the woods. This is a peaceful stretch with pools of grass and summer wildflowers surrounding the base of big trees. When it reconnects with Mount Lemmon Trail, turn left back to the trailhead, 1.6 miles total.

Unusual rocky designs line the Sky Island Parkway as it climbs from desert to cool forest. Courtesy of Rick Mortensen, Cincinnati.

BUTTERFLY TRAIL #16

This trail makes a wonderful introduction to the diversity of these mountains. It's been designated a Research Natural Area, and yes, it often swarms with butterflies. It would be over 11 miles round trip if you completed the entire trail, but unless you're in training, just sample a portion. The lower trailhead is at the Palisades Visitor Center but continue 4 miles up the highway to Soldier Camp Access Road. From this upper trailhead, the path makes a fairly gentle descent for the first 1.25 miles through hushed forest adorned with the wildflowers that attract the butterflies. Go as far as you like and turn around. Crystal Springs Trail enters at the 1.4-mile mark, if you need a definitive turnaround point.

Information for all hiking trails: (520) 749-8700, www.fs.usda.gov/coronado.

Where to Eat and Stay

TUCSON TAMALE CO., TUCSON

Restaurants that specialize need to deliver the goods on their signature item. Tucson Tamale Co. does that with two restaurants and several stores carrying their products. Order at the counter and in a blink you're unwrapping a warm cornhusk to find a moist steamy tamale inside. The masa swaddling the ingredients is soft and flavorful. The blue corn tamale bursting with squash, corn, tomato, and cheese is a favorite. Everything is vividly fresh. Choose from meaty, veggie, and vegan varieties. They make burritos, too. You can also order frozen tamales to enjoy at home. 7159 E. Tanque Verde Rd., (520) 298-8404, www.tucson tamale.com.

PREP & PASTRY, TUCSON

Prep & Pastry is reminiscent of a French farmhouse, open and airy with bare wood tables and high ceilings of exposed rafters. Since opening in 2013, they've gone about reimagining breakfast. Drawing raves are dishes like the Sweet Potato Hash, caramelized diced sweet potatoes mixed with corn, bell peppers, asparagus, and a delicate herbed mousse—and wearing a chapeau of over-easy eggs. Even traditional menu items come with a twist. The biscuit and gravy, for example, is a herbed cheddar biscuit with duck-fat gravy. The lunch menu receives the same funky spin. 2660 N. Campbell Ave., (520) 326-7737, www .prepandpastry.com.

LODGE ON THE DESERT, TUCSON

Dating back to the 1930s, Lodge on the Desert is situated on five shady acres in midtown. The hacienda-style accommodations are exactly the kind of Tucson experience you hope to find. Choose between the vintage charm of historic Casita rooms or the more modern Deluxe rooms done in Southwestern style. A complementary hot Sonoran breakfast gets your day started right. 306 N. Alvernon Way, (520) 320-2000, www.lodgeonthedesert.com.

When You Go

Visit Tucson: 115 N. Church Ave., (520) 624-1817, www.visittucson.org.

Santa Catalina Ranger District: (520) 749-8700, www.fs.usda.gov/coronado.

Rose Canyon Lake: (520) 576-3091.

Mt. Lemmon General Store & Gift Shop: (520) 576-1468, www.mtlemmon.com.

Ski Valley: (520) 576-1321, www.skithe lemmon.com.

Organ Pipe Cactus National Monument protects a swath of pristine desert including a large population of the namesake cactus. Photo by the author.

Organ Pipe Cactus Parkway

Overview This road travels north to south through the remote and biologically diverse Organ Pipe Cactus National Monument, west of Tucson.

Route Numbers Arizona State Highway 85.

Mileage The scenic road is 21 miles (Milepost 57 to Milepost 78). Organ Pipe Cactus National Monument is located approximately 125 miles from both Phoenix and Tucson.

Special Notes Organ Pipe Cactus National Monument shares 31 miles of international border with Mexico. Always be aware of your surroundings. If you see any activity that looks illegal, suspicious, or out of place, do not intervene. Note your location. Call 911 or report it to a ranger as quickly as possible.

We take our desert seriously in Arizona. We're the only state with a national park *and* a national monument dedicated to the protection of cactus. While plenty of folks explore the two segments of Saguaro National Park bracketing Tucson, far fewer have ventured to the remote outpost of Organ Pipe Cactus National Monument.

Organ Pipe sits on the border with Mexico, far enough away from population centers to only receive a trickle of visitors. Yet the monument preserves over 500 square miles of pristine Sonoran Desert. Gentle valleys that bristle with forests of saguaros stretch between ranges of craggy mountains. Over 90 percent of the terrain is designated wilderness.

All told, twenty-eight species of cactus can be found in the park, including the namesake organ pipe. Unlike the stately saguaro that rises in a single trunk, the organ pipe is a furious clutter of segments

Travel Note Why is not the only Arizona oddity. Other towns across the state are named Nothing, Surprise, Show Low, Carefree, Bumble Bee, Skull Valley, Chloride, Tombstone, Bagdad, and Tuba City.

shooting up from the base, a cactus forever in celebratory mode—throwing its arms in the air like it just doesn't care. A striking resemblance to the pipes of a church organ prompted its moniker. The monument is one of the few spots where the large cactus grows in this country.

The parkway begins on Arizona 85, just south of Why, a wisp of a town near the western border of the Tohono O'odham Indian Reservation. Such a great name for a town, but it's hard to tell whether it sprang from a simple lack of imagination by the town's founders, or maybe a sly sense of humor. Ostensibly, Why was named for the old Y intersection formed by Arizona 85 and Arizona 86. Perhaps it also was in response to their own internal query as to why they had chosen to settle in such a remote spot. The junction was later changed to a T-configuration.

Five miles south of Why the road enters Organ Pipe Cactus National Monument. President Franklin Delano Roosevelt declared Organ Pipe a national monument in 1937. For decades, the park has been showcasing plants and animals of the Sonoran Desert. The years of added protection are evident in the towering groves of saguaros that have been allowed to flourish, the hordes of organ pipes crowding the slopes, and numerous other species that have found a home here.

In 1976, the United Nations recognized the diversity of the monument by naming it an International Biosphere Reserve. The designation has attracted scientists from around the world conducting studies on this intact Sonoran Desert ecosystem.

Recent history has been less kind to Organ Pipe. In the 1990s border-security crackdowns in urban areas sent human and drug traffickers into the rural outback seeking new routes from Mexico to the United States. The monument became a thoroughfare for illegal activity, culminating in 2002 when park ranger Kris Eggle was shot and killed by drug smugglers. After that, most of what was deemed America's "most dangerous national park" was closed to the public.

In the ensuing years, numerous security measures have been implemented. Miles of vehicle barriers were installed along with surveillance towers and pedestrian fences. Additional law enforcement rangers were added to the monument's staff, and Border Patrol dramatically beefed up their presence. Now park rangers strive to educate visitors so they can make informed decisions about where to explore. In September 2015, all of Organ Pipe's 516 square miles were once again opened to hikers, campers, birders, and desert lovers.

Don't expect any kind of driving challenge. There are no twists and turns; the road slices south in a long straight line through the broad Valley of the Ajo. These are big wide-open spaces framed by the Bates Mountains in the west, the Puerto Blanco Mountains to the south, and the Ajo Range in the east.

Of all Arizona's officially designated scenic roads, this is the only one that beats with a desert heart. It climbs to no higher elevations, visits no lakes, and passes through no forests, canyons, or towns. It offers only a pleasing array of cactus, rocky terrain, and vast sky. For me, that's more than enough.

It's the silence that first grabs your attention. That's the plain simple music of Organ Pipe. Noise has no penetrative power across this broad desert. This is the place for anyone looking to escape the general hubbub of civilization. I've camped in the monument a few times and honestly believe it is one of the quietest places I've ever been.

Start at the Kris Eggle Visitor Center, named to honor the fallen park ranger. There's a gift shop inside along with interpretive exhibits and a short video presentation. Rangers can answer any questions. They conduct daily talks, guided walks, van tours, and other programs during winter months.

Located near the south end of the park, most activities revolve around the visitor center. The Twin Peaks Campground with its network of trails is nearby. Two rugged scenic drives that probe the backcountry of Organ Pipe depart from here.

Travel Note Organ pipe cactus may live to be 150 years old and reach an average height of 15 feet. Each summer lesser long-nosed bats migrate from Mexico to feast on the nectar of the cactus flowers.

The Ajo Mountain Drive is a 21-mile one-way loop that puts some of the park's best scenery on display. The graded gravel road, suitable for sedans, climbs from the valley floor into the foothills of the Ajo Mountains. It skirts past carved canyons and sharp cliffs. Picnic tables and hiking trails are accessible along the route. Don't miss this drive.

The other popular roadway is the Puerto

Hikers take a winter walk on the Victoria Mine Trail. Photo by the author.

Blanco Drive. This 37-mile loop circles Puerto Blanco Mountains and offers expansive views. A half day is required to make the full drive, and a 4WD is required for certain segments. But visitors can reach Pinkley Peak Picnic Area as a short out-and-back on the north side.

Organ Pipe is bordered by the small towns of Why on the northern edge and Lukeville to the south, the entry point to Mexico. Each community offers gas, a convenience store, and a restaurant. Lodging is available in Ajo, a former mining town 16 miles north of the park. While Ajo is still trying to find its way forward following the loss of the large copper mine that closed in 1984, it seems to be moving in a good direction with a focus on the arts and restoration of historic architecture.

The graceful town plaza is a centerpiece project in Ajo. The Spanish Colonial Revival–style plaza surrounds a park of green lawn and tall palm trees. Anchored at one end by the old train depot, now housing the visitor center, an eclectic collection of shops fills in the other two sides of the square with arched walkways and a continuous red tile roof. Directly across from the plaza are two whitewashed mission-style churches, almost blinding in the desert sun.

A block away, the historic Curley School has been renovated into live-work space apartments for a community of artists. The presence of so many creative folk may explain the colorful murals, both historic and fanciful, splashed on walls throughout the town. My personal favorite is a tribute to the 1972 horror thriller *Night of the Lepus*, which was filmed in the area. In this cult classic, Stuart Whitman, Rory Calhoun, and DeForest Kelley battle deranged killer—wait for it—bunny rabbits. And if that doesn't make you reach for the popcorn, you and I are very different people.

Ajo is one of those towns I'm always rooting for. There's so much old-world charm plopped down in the middle of the desert. It makes a great base camp for an Organ Pipe visit.

As a final note, it's not my intention to downplay any potential dangers of visiting the national monument. The possibility of encountering illegal activity is real. I just don't think it's very likely, especially after all the safety measures that have been implemented. Migrants and smugglers want to avoid detection and tend to steer clear of roads and trails. From a personal standpoint, I've visited Organ Pipe several times through the years. I've pitched my tent in the campground and in the backcountry (astonishing night skies), driven the rough scenic roads, and hiked the trails. Not once have I stumbled on illegal activity.

Be knowledgeable, alert, and prepared. Of course, those are good rules for any adventure you undertake. Then consider exploring the pristine and remarkable desert country of Organ Pipe Cactus National Monument.

Hiking

ESTES CANYON–BULL PASTURE LOOP

This rugged 3.1-mile loop is probably the best known of Organ Pipe's hiking trails. It leaves from the Estes Canyon Picnic Area, the midpoint of the Ajo Mountain Drive. Almost immediately, the route splits. Bear right on Bull Pasture Trail and climb to the top of a ridge in a series of switchbacks. You'll gain over 800 feet but the far-reaching views will hold your attention. You'll pass a second junction with Estes Canyon Trail, but continue up a higher slope to an overlook gazing across the basin surrounded by mountains. Ranchers used to graze their cattle in this pasture. An unofficial trail climbs to Mount Ajo, at 4,808 feet the highest peak in the monument. Proceed with extreme caution if you continue on this exposed path. Return via Estes Canyon Trail, dropping steeply before leveling out.

VICTORIA MINE TRAIL

Leading from the south side of the monument's campground, this 2.2-mile trail rambles across a desert plain to the foothills of the Sonoyta Mountains. The trail shows off the range of cactus species the park protects as it drops in and out of arroyos and makes its way to the remains of the Victoria Mine. Dating back to the 1890s, the Victoria produced enough gold and silver to keep men digging for decades in this lonely place. Rusting equipment lies scattered about, and the ruins of the company store still stand. Return the way you came or continue on one of the other trails connecting here.

ARCH CANYON TRAIL

An easy, short (0.6 miles) path leads into the mouth of a canyon on the west side of the Ajo Mountains. A 90-foot-wide arch breaks apart the cliffs near the top of the canyon wall. Views of the span are best early on. As the trail climbs up the ravine, the arch disappears, but vistas down canyon grow more expansive. At the end of the maintained trail, a strenuous unofficial route scrambles higher. Use caution, as footing can be dicey. Arch Canyon is located off the Ajo Mountain Drive.

Information for all hiking trails: (520) 387-6849, www.nps.gov/orpi.

Where to Eat and Stay

100 ESTRELLA RESTAURANT, AJO

This funky little place occupies a cool historic building in downtown Ajo, across from the town plaza. They serve big juicy burgers and fresh salads, and keep a surprising selection of craft beers on tap. 100 W. Estrella Ave., (520) 387-3110.

SONORAN DESERT INN AND CONFERENCE CENTER, AJO

This place is a happy desert surprise. Classrooms at the old elementary school have been converted into lovely accommodations. The inn is wrapped around a spacious courtyard overlooking full gardens. Guestrooms are done in a contemporary Southwestern style with natural light streaming through tall windows. The inn is operated by the nonprofit International Sonoran Desert Alliance, the same group that restored the town plaza. 55 Orilla Ave., (520) 373-0804, www.sonorandesertconferencecenter.com.

LA SIESTA MOTEL & RV RESORT, AJO

Sitting just a bit north of town, this classic motor court features rooms that are spotlessly clean and boasting some surprising amenities like tile floors and large flat-screen televisions. They have standalone cabins, a secluded pool and hot tub, a tennis court, and RV park. But be aware they don't allow children under ten. 2561 N. Ajo Gila Bend Highway, (602) 975-0106, www.ajolasiesta.com.

When You Go

Organ Pipe Cactus National Monument: Fee. (520) 387-6849, www.nps.gov/orpi.
Ajo District Chamber of Commerce: 1 W. Plaza St., (520) 387-7742, www.ajochamber.com.

Patagonia–Sonoita Scenic Road

Overview Showing off a surprising side of Southern Arizona, this road flows between the Santa Rita and Patagonia Mountains, across rangy grasslands where wineries are tucked among the rolling hills, and riparian corridors attract more than three hundred species of bird.

Route Numbers Arizona State Highways 82 and 83.

Mileage The scenic road is 52.5 miles (Milepost 4.5 to Milepost 32, and Milepost 33 to Milepost 58). It is 80 miles from Tucson to Nogales and 146 miles round trip if you return via Interstate 19.

Special Notes Allow yourself plenty of time to take in all the sights on this drive.

Here's one of my absolute favorite pieces of Arizona trivia: The movie *Oklahoma!* was filmed here.

When Curly McLain sang about the "bright golden haze on the meadow," he was describing Arizona. Filmmakers couldn't find enough undeveloped land in the Sooner State, so they chose the windswept grasslands of Santa Cruz County as a more suitable location. That has to be a burr under the saddle of Oklahomans. I can't imagine going to see a big budget production called *Arizona!* that was filmed in Delaware with a culvert full of Styrofoam boulders passing as the Grand Canyon.

The best part is that they could come back and film it again in the exact same locations that are still part of a vast open tract of land. Or they could shoot a sequel: *Oklahoma 2: Jud's Revenge.*

I like to surprise people with this drive.

Late-afternoon light stretches across the golden plains toward the hamlet of Elgin. Photo by the author.

Pastoral grasslands, vineyards, and hidden lakes are among the last things people expect to find in Southern Arizona, just miles from the Mexican border.

The road starts in sure-enough desert, leaving Interstate 10 at Exit 281 about 20 miles east of Tucson. Head south on Arizona 83 amid ocotillo scrubland, mixed with prickly pear, barrel cactus, and mesquite trees. After a few miles the road climbs through a rugged canyon. The Empire Mountains rise to the east, and the mighty Santa Rita Mountains loom on the western side.

Travel Note Other movies that have been filmed in the region include *The Outlaw Josie Wales*, *Red River*, *Tom Horn*, *The Postman*, *Hombre*, *Last Train from Gun Hill*, and *McClintock!*

It begins to feel like a mountain drive as you continue winding up through the canyon gazing across brushy ridgelines to the slopes beyond. Then the road bends to the southeast and things change. You begin crossing a virtual sea of grass.

Sprinkled with oak trees and lightly carved by stream channels that are mostly dry, this is part of the vast Sonoita Plain. It's a delicious horizon-stretching expanse of soft undulating hills that seems to go on forever. Arizona contains several distinctive, instantly recognizable features like the Grand Canyon, Monument Valley, and Sedona's red rocks. The Sonoita Plain should be included in that list.

Champagne-colored grasses sway at the

More than 100 shops and galleries line the shady streets in the village of Tubac. Courtesy of Rick Mortensen, Cincinnati.

touch of every breeze. Mountains that once dominated are shoved back by this unexpected savanna. When Curly McLain sang about a meadow, he was dangerously underselling it. This is prairie. This is a land built for covered wagons and bison herds. These are wide-open spaces where the Old West still lives and breathes. If God has a lawn, this is it.

The Las Cienegas Natural Conservation Area (NCA) protects more than 45,000 acres of grasslands as well as the riparian corridor of Cienega Creek. The perennial stream gets its name from the cienegas, or marshes, that occur along its length. The heart of the NCA is historic Empire Ranch. You'll spot the turnoff for the ranch near Milepost 40. Head east for 3 miles where you'll find a collection of buildings, mostly old adobes.

Empire Ranch dates back to the 1870s, and during its heyday was one of the largest in Arizona. The clustered ranch buildings overlook a shallow wash lined by cottonwood trees. There is informational signage scattered among the structures and a half-mile walking path leads you back to the gallery of cottonwoods. There's usually a docent on site, and guided tours of the ranch headquarters are conducted the second and fourth Saturday of every month. The Bureau of Land Management manages both the ranch and the NCA, but the nonprofit Empire Ranch Foundation provides funds and volunteers to help preserve the ranch.

You can continue deeper into Las Cienegas NCA, but within a few miles the road turns challenging, generally requiring 4WD.

Back on 83, it's about 10 miles to Sonoita, which is more crossroads than town. This is where Arizona 83 and Arizona 82 intersect and the handful of businesses—gas station, general store, restaurants, and inns—are all strung along the highway. But there's so much more than meets the eye.

This is the cradle of Arizona's wine

industry. It all sprang from these sun-drenched hills pressed beneath an immense sprawling sky. In the late 1970s, a University of Arizona soil scientist, Gordon Dutt, found the soil in the area to be strikingly similar to that in Burgundy, France. He planted the first grapes in 1979 and opened Sonoita Vineyards in 1983.

Today, a dozen or so wineries dot the hills, most of them in the even smaller burg of Elgin, 9 miles east of Sonoita. These are family-owned vineyards producing a wide range of varietals. A handful of wineries and wine-tasting rooms are open on weekdays, but you'll have more to sample on weekends when everyone is pouring.

Continuing on the scenic drive, Sonoita marks the end of the journey on Arizona 83. Turn right on Arizona 82 proceeding southwest. There's a historical marker commemorating Camp Crittenden, an active military post from 1867 to 1873 established to protect settlements against Indian attacks.

About a dozen miles from Sonoita, Patagonia nestles in a long green valley. Assorted historic buildings house shops, galleries, and eateries all surrounding the big community park that anchors downtown. The picturesque setting makes Patagonia a beloved destination for road trippers. While Sonoita and Elgin are defined by the wineries, Patagonia has sown more eclectic oats offering a little something for everyone. The tree-lined hamlet is known as an arts community, a haven for birders, and a hotspot for butterflies—possibly the most charming triple threat ever.

On the edge of town you'll find a couple of spots frequented by birders. The Tucson Audubon's Paton Center for Hummingbirds is a simple home site filled with feeders, flowers, and fountains that attract all sorts of winged visitors. Right next door is the Patagonia–Sonoita Creek Preserve (see Hiking).

A few miles south of Patagonia is the turnoff for Patagonia Lake State Park. Tucked away amid sloping hills, the 250-acre lake offers boating, fishing, waterskiing, camping, and a sandy swimming beach. Boat rentals are available. The park also provides access to the Sonoita Creek State Natural Area and over 20 miles of hiking trails (see Hiking).

A few more miles crossing grassy ridges, skirting small canyons with nice views of the Patagonia Mountains, and the road ends in Nogales. This is the largest border city in Arizona and the international entry point into Nogales, Mexico.

You can return the way you came because there's plenty to see all over again. The other option is to travel north to Tucson via Interstate 19. Now I'm a firm believer in the mathematical theorem: the fewer the lanes of highway, the greater the chance for adventure. So I don't normally advocate interstates as part of the travel experience. But there are so many attractions, both scenic and historic, spread along I-19 that it's worth the journey.

Stops worth considering along I-19 include Pena Blanca Lake, Tumacácori National Historical Park, Tubac Presidio State Historic Park, the arts village of Tubac, Titan Missile Museum, Madera Canyon, and San Xavier Mission. And bonus: distances on I-19 are signed in kilometers, not miles. How often do you get to see that?

Travel Note The best months for birding at Patagonia–Sonoita Creek Preserve are March through September.

More Scenic Driving

Enjoy more of the heart-stealing scenery of the Sonoita Plain when you continue on Arizona 83 through Elgin and on to Parker

Canyon Lake. It may even be prettier and is certainly more rustic. From Sonoita, instead of turning onto Arizona 82, proceed southeast to Elgin on Arizona 83 where you'll enjoy the familiar grasslands sprouting oak and mesquite. This is where you'll find a collection of vineyards and wineries. As you leave the grapevines in your rearview mirror, you'll see more cattle grazing and tidy ranch houses. The road turns narrower and dips and curves through the Canelo Hills. It's 30 miles to Parker Canyon Lake, full of resident bass, sunfish, catfish, and stocked rainbow trout. The 130-acre lake sits amid soft hills at 5,400 feet and includes a campground and small store with boat rentals.

In Nogales, a statue commemorates Father Eusebio Kino, an early Jesuit missionary and explorer of the Southwest. Courtesy of Rick Mortensen, Cincinnati.

Hiking

PATAGONIA-SONOITA CREEK PRESERVE

The Nature Conservancy stepped in to protect a stretch of Sonoita Creek at the edge of Patagonia and the verdant floodplain adjacent to the stream as their very first project in Arizona. Over three hundred bird species migrate, nest, and live amid this rare and beautiful Fremont cottonwood–Gooding's willow riparian forest. There are several gentle paths you can take including one along the old railroad grade, another that follows the creek, and a mile-long connector to the Paton Center for Hummingbirds. If you want to stretch your legs a little more, the Geoffrey Platts Trail makes a 3.2-mile loop through mesquite-covered hills with views of the mountains and valley. Fee. (520) 394-2400, www.nature.org.

OVERLOOK TRAIL

The Patagonia Lake State Park oversees the adjacent Sonoita Creek State Natural Area (SCSNA), which preserves the fragile riparian watershed. While it remains completely undeveloped, more than 20 miles of hiking trails amble down to the stream and cut across the rolling hills. Access to the natural area is through Patagonia Lake State Park, where you'll receive a permit. From the SCSNA parking area the Overlook Trail (1.4 miles round trip) climbs the slope of a standalone hill sprinkled with ocotillos. On top is a shaded bench where you can sit and relax and savor the impressive views of the lake, framed by mountains. Fee. (520) 287-6965, www.azstateparks.com.

MT. WRIGHTSON

After gazing at the Santa Rita Mountains for much of this drive, you may get the urge to climb to the top of them. If you're returning by way of I-19, you'll have that chance. Two trails—Old Baldy #372 and Super Trail #134—form a figure eight, allowing for different route options as they make their way to the 9,543-foot summit of Mt. Wrightson. Baldy is shorter and shadier but steeper while Super sees a little less foot traffic. It will be a strenuous hike no matter which route you take, but you'll enjoy some great views even if you don't go all the way to the top. Take the Madera Canyon Exit off I-19 and drive 13.5 miles on Madera Canyon Road to the Roundup Picnic Area. Turn left here and drive to the trailhead. Fee. (520) 281-2296, www.fs.usda.gov/coronado.

Where to Eat and Stay

THE CAFÉ, SONOITA

At this comfortably hip eatery, you'll find a strong local influence from the wines to the chef, both of which were made right here in the 'hood. Chef Adam Puckle was born nearby and went to school in Elgin and Patagonia. He left just long enough to study the culinary arts in college. One of the intriguing menu items is the APE Burger, which stands for Adam Puckle Experience. Tell your server if you have any food allergies and then sit back as the chef whips up a one-of-a-kind specialty. 3280 Arizona 82, (520) 455-5044, www.cafesonoita.com.

COCINA LA LEY, NOGALES

Step into the Nogales restaurant and you'll feel like you wandered a few blocks further south and are dining across the border. Authentic food is made using fresh natural ingredients at this family-owned eatery. Tacos and soups make up the menu, an excellent variety of each. Meat, fish, or shrimp comes wrapped in a warm tortilla, and then you pile on the extras from the well-stocked salsa bar. The fresh seafood soup with a slightly spicy broth is a house favorite. 226 W. 3rd St., (520) 287-4555, www.cocinalaley.com.

STAGE STOP INN, PATAGONIA

In 1969, local ranchers built the Stage Stop in downtown Patagonia. Part of the reason for the inn was to accommodate their friend John Wayne and cast and crew members that were filming movies in the area. Homey, comfortable rooms feature unique details, and some include kitchenettes. There's a swimming pool, a shady courtyard, a reading lounge, game room, and a restaurant on premises. Some of the second-floor rooms overlook the town park. 303 W. McKeown Ave., (520) 394-2211, www.stagestoppatagonia.com.

When You Go

Empire Ranch: (888) 364-2829, www.empireranchfoundation.org.

Las Cienegas National Conservation Area: (520) 258-7200, www.blm.gov/visit/las-cienegas.

Sonoita–Elgin Chamber of Commerce: www.sonoitaelginchamber.org.

Sky Islands Tourism Association: Patagonia Regional Visitor Center, corner of Third and McKeown, (520) 394-7750, www.patagoniaaz.com.

Tucson Audubon's Paton Center for Hummingbirds: 447 Pennsylvania Ave., (520) 415-6447.

Nogales-Santa Cruz County Chamber of Commerce: 123 W. Kino Park, Nogales, (520) 287-3685, www.thenogaleschamber.org.

Parker Canyon Lake: (520) 455-5847, www.parkercanyonlake.com.

The Swift Trail makes a twisting climb up the slopes of Mt. Graham, southern Arizona's highest peak. Photo by the author.

Swift Trail Parkway

Overview The road climbs steeply up the forested flanks of Mount Graham, gaining over 6,000 feet in elevation, and providing access to a recreational bounty of hiking, biking, camping, and fishing.

Route Numbers Arizona State Highway 366.

Mileage The parkway is 26 miles (Milepost 116 to Milepost 142). It's 35 miles to the end of the road near the top of Mount Graham.

Special Notes Expect mountain grades, hairpin turns, and sharp drop-offs. The last 12 miles are a narrow, winding gravel road passable to sedans. Due to the sharp curves it is not recommended for vehicles over 26 feet long. The upper portion of the road, about where the pavement ends, is closed from November 15 to April 15. The mountain sustained damage in the lightning-caused Frye Fire that burned 48,000 acres in June and July 2017.

Soon as I started to fall, I twisted and tucked in to avoid landing on my head or spine.

It worked because I hit hard just below my left shoulder blade, then slid down the steep stone banks ending up in the creek. Somehow—and I'm still not sure how—I scraped my left leg on the way down because the shin was bleeding from several ugly looking gashes. I hobbled back to the rental car to assess the damage.

I was 9,000 feet up on the side of Mount Graham on a dirt road, deep in bear country. I was bloody, soaking wet, and gasping for breath. But otherwise, my journey up the Swift Trail had been a blast.

Travel Note Mount Graham is home to a subspecies of red squirrels, once thought to be extinct but rediscovered in the 1970s. The squirrel was added to the federally endangered species list in 1987 when the estimated population was fewer than four hundred.

Lately, it had occurred to me that sky islands are the essence of Arizona. They are one of the things that define us, forested peaks rising from the desert, diverse habitats in close proximity—the hot and the cool practically side by side. And nowhere in the state is that connection on such dramatic display as the Pinaleno Mountains.

The Pinalenos in southeastern Arizona have over 7,000 feet of vertical relief, more than any other range in the state. They are topped by Mount Graham, at 10,720 feet, the highest mountain in Southern Arizona. The Swift Trail begins south of Safford in desert scrubland and makes a winding drive into the high forests on the slope of Graham.

While the Swift Trail is similar to the Sky Island Parkway climbing to the top of Mount Lemmon in Tucson, there are differences. Sky Island is a wider, smoother road with passing lanes and pullouts built to accommodate heavy traffic and bicyclists. Guardrails make it seem more secure. The Swift Trail feels raw and intimate. It's a narrower road, a country road, with sharp twists and turns, and unpaved at the top. It may also be the most inappropriately named highway in Arizona because swift it is not, as it makes a tortured switchbacking ascent up the flanks of the mountain. This is a curvy, swervy, skyscraping road, and one that's almost entirely without a guardrail.

When I planned my trip to this corner of the state I knew I was going to be driving the Swift Trail, a journey I hadn't made for many years. For some reason the thought gave me pause. Every time I pondered that drive I felt a sense of low-grade foreboding. I spend enough time alone in wild country to listen to my instincts. My faithful but creaky old pickup had developed a curious rattle recently, so I decided to leave it home and rented a car. Problem solved, I figured.

The drive passes through five of North America's seven life zones, encompassing a wide range of plant and animal life. From Safford, a small farming and ranching community, head south for 7 miles on US 191 and then turn right onto Arizona 366. A half-mile down the road you'll pass Mt. Graham Market, a last chance for supplies. You'll find no amenities on the mountain.

The road runs straight and level for the first couple of miles but that doesn't last. It rises from the cactus, yucca, and mesquite and soon climbs into rising grasslands and then into sharper-edged hills dotted with oak and pine as it enters Coronado National Forest.

At about 7 miles, I reached the Noon Creek Picnic Area with tables and grills tucked amid the trees. Back in the horse-and-wagon days, travelers would usually arrive at this shady spot in time for the mid-day meal, inspiring the name.

As you climb, the road passes a turnoff to the historic Angle Orchard where fruit can be purchased in late summer and early autumn. A sign is posted at the road junction if fruit is available. A small creek splashes through dense forest at the cozy Wet Canyon Picnic Area. Arcadia Campground is the first of a half-dozen national forest campgrounds on the mountain. The switchbacks and hairpin curves seem to come faster now climbing into stands of Chiricahua and ponderosa pines. The Ladybug Saddle perches at 8,500 feet and is named for the large number of the colorful insects that gather here during summer.

The pavement gives way to graded dirt

Travel Note The Pinaleno Mountains are reported to have the west's largest concentration of black bears.

after 23 miles. There's a gate here that's closed during winter months. I stopped at Hospital Flat, an appealing meadow sliced by a skinny stream. As I walked toward a short nature trail, two wild turkeys headed for the trees. The meadow was once used as a hospital during the summer heat by soldiers from Fort Grant, at the base of the mountain.

There's plenty of history here, including a trail to Heliograph Peak. It was used as an Army heliograph station in the late 1800s. Signals were given by sunlight flashing on large mirrors across Southern Arizona. Legend has it that Treasure Park is where Mexican banditos buried a fortune in gold and silver.

The Civilian Conservation Corps built much of the Swift Trail during the Great Depression. The road was named for Theodore Swift, supervisor of Crook National Forest (now Coronado National Forest) from 1908 to 1923. Columbine Visitor Information Center (at about Mile 29) is open on weekends May through September.

Near the road's terminus, I pulled over to explore a sparkling body of water. Riggs Flat Lake sits in a bowl at 8,600 feet ringed by pine and fir trees. The dam used to form the eleven-acre lake was built in 1957. Stocked with rainbow, brown, and brook trout, Riggs Flat Lake has become a popular fishing and camping spot. Small boats are permitted, but most fish from the shoreline. There's an adjacent campground with tables, fire grills, and vault toilets. An easy trail circles the lake and another leads to a viewpoint.

The Swift Trail doesn't end at the summit, which is crowned by the Mount Graham International Observatory, containing some of the largest telescopes in the world. The controversial project was built in the 1990s, despite the efforts of environmentalists seeking to protect the endangered red squirrel and the Apache Indians who consider the mountain a sacred place. The observatory is only open to the public via daylong tours beginning in Safford at the Eastern Arizona College Discovery Park Campus. Tours are conducted mid-May through October (weather permitting) and include a sack lunch.

The Swift Trail continues for another mile to the Clark Peak Corrals but since I am sans horse, I turned around and began my descent. Still alert to potential danger, I drove very cautiously.

After a few miles I pulled over at Post Creek where a clear stream spilled down a cliff face. I scrambled up the rocks to snap a few photos. On the way down, I stepped closer to the creek for one last shot. Suddenly my right foot lost purchase, and I went flying over backward.

When I hit, all the wind gushed out of me. I slid down the rocky face through the flow of water. Back at the car, I dug out my first-aid kit, which, I discovered, lacked some essential items due to years of disuse. I doctored my leg the best I could with a tiny alcohol swab and made my way back down the mountain. I had to forego a couple of planned hikes but made it back to Safford without further incident.

As a postscript, I was sore for three weeks but sustained no lasting damage. I've since upgraded my first-aid kit and double-checked all my emergency supplies. I still listen to my instincts. They served me well in this case, warning me of possible perils on the Swift Trail. Unfortunately, I was too focused on the drive and didn't exercise proper caution elsewhere. That was carelessness on my part. Overall, it was a good reminder that sometimes travel doesn't go as planned. It's wise to be prepared and alert when rambling in back-country.

As a final postscript, about a month after my adventure on the Swift Trail, a lightning strike ignited a fire on the slopes of Mount Graham. The Frye Fire would go on to burn 48,000 acres before being contained in July 2017.

A postfire analysis found about 5 percent of the landscape received a rating of high-burn severity, about 12 percent as moderate-burn severity and the rest as low-burn severity. Much of the damage took place away from the road, but there will be a few scars and some trails will be impacted. The observatory emerged unscathed but the endangered Mount Graham red squirrel did not fare as well. The population had declined since the observatory was built. It was estimated at 252 before the fire and only 35 in the months afterward. The animals are being carefully monitored to see if they can come back from the brink of extinction yet again.

Hiking

GRANT HILL LOOP #322

The forest service did a nice job putting together an interconnected route designed with mountain biking in mind. It also happens to offer some of the most enjoyable hiking on the mountain. They combine a collection of old logging roads (closed to vehicles) and link them with single-track trails to form a series of loops. Easiest travel is in a clockwise direction as you pass through mixed conifer forests interspersed with small meadows. It's 4.2 miles if you stick to the wide outer loop, but you can increase your mileage by taking some of the internal segments. Trailhead for Grant Hill is a half-mile past Hospital Flat on the left

Nestled in the forest at 8,600 feet, Riggs Flat Lake makes a refreshing summer getaway. Photo by the author.

side of the road. The Cunningham Loop #316 sits on the right side of the road and can be added to the mix.

WEBB PEAK TRAIL #345

This relatively short trail leads to the Webb Peak Lookout where you'll enjoy some far-reaching views. It leaves from the public corrals across from the Columbine Visitor Information Center and reaches the tower after a mile. Easiest return is via the Webb Peak Road. Or you can connect with the Ash Creek Trail #307 and return to the corrals that way, about a 2.8-mile loop.

SHAKE TRAIL #309

The upper trailhead is about a mile past Ladybug Saddle on the left. It descends from the forested slopes to the oak and juniper savannah near Stockton Pass. It will be a 10-mile round trip if you complete it, so you may just want to sample a portion. There will be vistas of the Greasewood Mountains and Sulphur Springs Valley as you amble downhill. Wildlife is plentiful along the Shake Trail, primarily mule deer, but black bear are often seen as well.

Information for all hiking trails: (928) 428-4150, www.fs.usda.gov/coronado.

Where to Eat and Stay

CASA MAÑANA, SAFFORD

This Safford landmark opened in 1951 and is one of the original Salsa Trail eateries. The Salsa Trail is a collection of mom-and-pop restaurants scattered across the communities of southeastern Arizona. A festive atmosphere and good food keep the regulars returning. Everybody has a favorite dish from the shredded beef tacos to the chile relleno topped with sweet onion sauce. But it's hard to go wrong with the creamy green chili chicken enchiladas. 502 S. First Ave., (928) 428-3170, www.thecasamanana.com.

TAYLOR FREEZE, PIMA

It all comes together at Taylor Freeze in Pima—the food, the friendly staff, and great retro vibe. The former Tastee Freeze has been family owned since 1968, dishing up burgers, sandwiches, chicken, and Mexican food. Everything is made fresh using quality ingredients. Of course, almost nobody walks out without dessert. There is a litany of flavors of soft-serve ice cream, and old-fashioned hand-blended sundaes and shakes. 225 W. Center St., (928) 485-2661.

COTTAGE BED AND BREAKFAST, SAFFORD

A lovely and spacious guest cottage with a bakery for a neighbor makes a great base camp to explore the region where there is plenty to see and do. It's on the property of the historic Olney House, a tall brick home built in 1890, named for a Graham County sheriff. The private cottage includes living room, kitchenette, bath, and bedroom with queen bed. A gourmet breakfast is served. 1104 South Central, (928) 428-5118, www.cottagebedandbreakfast.com.

When You Go

Graham County Chamber of Commerce: 1051 Thatcher Blvd., Safford, (928) 428-2511, www.grahamchamber.org.

Eastern Arizona College's Discovery Park Campus: 1651 W. Discovery Park Blvd., Safford, (928) 428-6260, www.eac.edu/discoverypark.

Historic Arizona US Route 80

Overview Fragments of old US 80 are scattered across Southern Arizona including the smile-shaped slice of Arizona 80 that explores a Wild West legacy.

Route Numbers Arizona State Highway 80, State Highway 77, State Highway 79, State Highway 79B, US 60, State Highway 85, and State Highway B8.

Mileage The historic road is 217.8 miles in varying segments. It is 122 miles from Benson to the Arizona–New Mexico state line along Arizona 80 as detailed in this chapter.

Special Notes Segments of Historic Arizona US Route 80 overlap the Gila-Pinal Scenic Road and Copper Corridor Scenic Road East.

Travel Note Due to the advent of interstate highways, all of US 80 was decommissioned west of Dallas, Texas, several years ago.

Although it never quite made the pop-culture splash as US 66, US 80 was a keystone highway in shaping American car culture. The cross-country thoroughfare once stretched from Savannah, Georgia, to San Diego, California, connecting the Atlantic and Pacific in a sunny all-weather route across southern states. Commissioned in 1926, it became known as the "Broadway of America." In September 2018, portions of old US 80 across Arizona were officially designated as a Historic Road.

Twisting through Arizona for 500 miles, the historic roadway linked small towns like Douglas, Gila Bend, and Yuma with the

The rising walls of the Chiricahua Mountains frame the road into Cave Creek Canyon. Photo by the author.

Plenty of Wild West history unfolded in the rugged lands of southeastern Arizona. Photo by the author.

urban centers of Tucson and Phoenix. Portions of the swooping route have been replaced by I-10 and Interstate 8, but long intact sections remain. Many of these are lined with historic motels, roadside attractions, neon signs, and iconic structures, the most notable being the Miracle Mile Historic District in Tucson. Others can be found in Mesa, Tempe, Phoenix, and Yuma. All are worth exploring, but for this chapter I'll focus on the 122 miles of Arizona State Highway 80 that curves through the southeastern corner of the state because it is a region that I dearly love.

When I've got a few vacation days in my pocket, this is where I come, the part of Arizona that intrigues me most. Cochise County dishes up a blend of history, scenery, and recreation that simply can't be matched.

This is a land of legends, where Apache warriors Cochise and Geronimo fought to preserve their way of life, and where Wyatt Earp and Doc Holliday shot their way into the history books. Here the edge of the Sonoran Desert brushes up against the fringe of the Chihuahuan Desert. Mountains rise from desert grasslands and the San Pedro River flows north forming a slender riparian corridor that helps make this one of the preeminent birding hotspots in the world.

One road links all the stories together.

Arizona 80 breaks off from I-10 at Exit 303 and angles south through Benson. The little town was a stopping point for the Butterfield Overland Stage and later a railroad hub. Mines at nearby Tombstone, Fairbank, Charleston, and Bisbee boomed, making this a crucial shipping center for ore and freight.

At the Benson Visitor Center, housed in the recreated railroad depot, they pay homage to their past in the best possible way—by playing with trains. Even better, they let you drive one. An AAR Control Stand looks like what you see in the cab of a real locomotive. Climb into the engineer's seat and operate throttle, brake, and whistle while piloting the G-scale Union Pacific SD 70 through the building on an elevated track. A mounted camera streams the journey. Anyone who can make it around the tracks without going all Casey Jones and causing a fiery crash is given a handsome certificate declaring them a Benson Train Engineer. I take mine with me every time I board a train as credentials, in case the engineer falls ill and they need a passenger to guide the big iron horse back to the station.

If your sweet tooth feels cranky, soothe it at Old Benson Ice Cream Stop, where they offer a kajillion flavors of soft serve. It opened as a Dairy Queen in 1953 but has been a simple neighborhood

Travel Note In Tucson, the historic alignment of 80 follows Oracle Road, Drachmann, Stone Avenue, South Sixth Avenue, and Benson Highway. There are many examples of classic mid-century architecture along the Miracle Mile, complemented by restored vintage neon signs.

mom-and-pop ice cream place for several years now. It's the kind of friendly let's-grab-a-cone joint every small town should have. Or wander across the street to the historic Horseshoe Café (open since 1936) for delicious homemade pie and pastries.

From Benson it's 24 miles to Tombstone. The road winds through ranchlands heavy with mesquite as it crosses the San Pedro River before passing through the farming community of St. David. The Dragoon Mountains rear up to the east, a long, narrow range crowned by granite boulders. These ramparts once provided refuge to Cochise and his band of Apaches. In the mountains, they could find food, water, and medicine, and had a commanding view of the valleys below making a surprise attack by the US Cavalry virtually impossible.

Tombstone sits on a wide plateau at an elevation of 4,500 feet. In 1877, prospector Ed Schiffelin discovered silver despite being warned he'd only find his tombstone in such wilderness. The town sprang up almost overnight and with so much sudden wealth being produced, it developed something of a cosmopolitan air. Along with saloons and brothels, there was an opera house, fine dining restaurants, luxury hotels, an ice cream parlor, and bowling alley.

Rolling into Tombstone, you pass one landmark and then another. On your left is Boothill Graveyard. Populated with colorful characters, this is the most famous cemetery of the Old West and well worth a respectful visit.

Next up is the site of the most famous shootout in western history, the true site. The gunfight that pitted the Earps and Doc Holliday against the Clantons and McLaurys did not take place in the O.K. Corral. It began in a narrow lot next to C. S. Fly's Photographic Studio on Fremont Street, a few doors west of the back entrance of the corral. In fact, much of the violence quickly spilled onto Fremont Street, known today as Highway 80. You'll pass a sign commemorating the gunfight site, which is now contained within the expanded O.K. Corral property.

Stagecoaches still clip-clop through Tombstone's historic downtown, and the twenty-minute narrated rides are a fun time. You can tour one of the original mines, grab a meal or beverage in a swinging-door saloon, and visit intriguing museums—including Tombstone Courthouse State Park, and the exquisitely preserved Bird Cage Theatre where 140 bullet holes still aerate the walls.

At the O.K. Corral reenactors wage the famous gun battle a few times each day. Visitors can also check out a blacksmith shop, C. S. Fly's studio and a gallery of his famous photographs, the boardinghouse where Doc Holliday roomed, and the spot where the shootout began.

South of Tombstone, the road crosses open country before climbing into the Mule Mountains. Oaks and sycamores spread across tilted slopes. Pass through a tunnel that feels like a portal somehow because when you emerge you're dropping

Travel Note In Yuma, US 80 traversed the Ocean to Ocean Bridge, crossing the Colorado River into California. Opened in 1915, it was the only vehicle bridge over the Colorado for 1,200 miles and made the southern transcontinental highway possible.

into the colorful sprawl of Bisbee, Arizona's most defiantly quirky town.

Blessed with a spectacular setting and old-world architectural flourishes, the former mining town has emerged as a multifaceted destination garnering national acclaim. Historic and funky, creaky and classy, Bisbee has evolved into a haven for artists.

In 1877, the first mining claims were filed in Bisbee where several rich ore bodies were discovered. Almost a century of mining—both underground and open pit—produced 8 billion pounds of copper, 102 million ounces of silver, and 2.8 million ounces of gold. When the last mine closed in the mid-1970s, much of Bisbee was abandoned. That's when folks of an artistic temperament moved in. Shops and galleries opened along narrow streets. Houses were refurbished, often set ablaze with color. Murals splashed across walls, and sculptures sprang up in tiny yards. Today, Bisbee's creative spirit proves infectious. This is where you come to experience art, to buy art, or to see life as an artist does. This is where you come for a jolt of inspiration.

Walk the hilly streets of the southernmost mile-high city in the nation. Dip in and out of the dozens of galleries that fill downtown. Visit a museum. Sign up for one of the paranormal experiences offered by Old Bisbee Ghost Tour, visiting everything from haunted hotels to haunted pubs. Or go underground to explore the Queen Mine Tour. You'll don hard hats and slickers to ride the mine train 1,500 feet into the depths. Tour guides are former miners who present an accurate and chilling portrayal of what the work was like.

Leaving Bisbee, the road skirts the rainbow-hued crater of the open pit. You soon reach a big roundabout where roads branch off like spokes from a wheel. It's about 26 miles to Douglas, perched on the Mexican border, originally founded as a smelter town to treat ores mined in Bisbee.

Travel Note Legend has it that Pancho Villa once rode his horse to the top of the marble staircase in the Gadsden Hotel, leaving a chip in the seventh step.

Although Douglas has seen better days, downtown is staging a modest comeback, led by the stunning Gadsden Hotel. Built in 1907, the stately four-story hotel features an unforgettable lobby. Four soaring marble columns flank a solid white Italian marble staircase. A massive stained glass mural covers one wall of the mezzanine and vaulted stained-glass skylights run the length of the lobby. Refurbished rooms and suites are being rented again but even if you're not spending the night, visit the restaurant or saloon, and be wowed by old-school grandeur.

Gas up before leaving Douglas. It's 47 miles to the state line as 80 twists through desert plains flanked by stark hills. Watch for a roadside pullout near the mouth of Skeleton Canyon about 9 miles from New Mexico. This stone pillar adorned with a plaque is the Geronimo Surrender Monument. In 1886, a weary and outnumbered Geronimo surrendered to General Nelson Miles, signaling an end to the Indian Wars in the Southwest. The actual surrender site lies deeper in Skeleton Canyon, now on private property.

The official historic road ends quietly at the New Mexico border, but that's not the end of the journey. Continue on 80 through the little burg of Rodeo, New Mexico. At the junction with Portal Road, you'll find the Chiricahua Desert Museum, housing a state-of-the-art live reptile exhibit, wildlife and botanical garden, art gallery, gift shop, and campground.

Turn west on Portal Road to reenter

Arizona where you'll plunge into a rare oasis. The road travels along the flanks of the Chiricahua Mountains, a ragged range sculpted by ancient volcanic activity. The hamlet of Portal consists of a lodge with a café (try the green chile cheeseburger) and small store. It guards the mouth of Cave Creek Canyon, known as "Arizona's Yosemite." Soaring cliffs rise above lush forests fed by a perennial stream. Majestic yet intimate, the canyon is a world-class birding destination.

The narrow road (Forest Road 42) winds beneath a canopy of trees, and cloud-spearing pinnacles of rhyolite rising overhead. The Cave Creek Visitor Information Center is manned by volunteers and offers information, maps, and current bird sightings.

The pavement ends just beyond the turnoff for South Fork Road, and you can return the way you came or continue on the dirt surface. FR 42 climbs higher into the mountains. You can make a loop by turning right on the graveled Paradise Road (FR 42B). When dry, this loop can usually be managed in a sedan. If you continue on FR 42, you'll cross the Onion Saddle on your way to Chiricahua National Monument, my secret garden.

Some of my very best days have been spent camping and hiking amid that wonderland of rocks. The twelve-thousand-acre monument contains an otherworldly display of sculpted stone. Massive columns, slender spires, and impossibly balanced boulders loom above the timber. The network of trails guides you through places of rare beauty. For me, it is a place of utter contentment. If only all road trips ended with such a flourish.

If you want to avoid a long dirt road drive, head back through Portal to Highway 80 in New Mexico. Drive north on 80 to I-10 and turn west to Willcox, Arizona. Take Arizona 186 south, following the signs to Chiricahua National Monument. Paved all the way. Plus, you can stop for a wine break in Willcox, with vineyards and wineries dotting the landscape.

Hiking

LOOP TRAIL

Settled in 1882, Fairbank was the closest rail stop to Tombstone. Today this is one of the best-preserved ghost towns in the area. A half-dozen structures huddle in the mesquite groves near the San Pedro River, including the schoolhouse that serves as a museum and visitor center on weekends. The 4-mile Loop Trail winds through the woods along the river, past the historic cemetery, and an old mill site. Fairbank Historic Site is located 10 miles west of Tombstone on Arizona 82. (520) 459-2555.

SOUTH FORK TRAIL #243

Whether you come for the birds or the scenery, this is a trail you don't want to miss. Located at the end of South Fork Road in Cave Creek Canyon, it follows an old roadbed to the creek, chasing the waterway through the defile. During spring mornings, don't be surprised to find birders staking out their favorite spot hoping to catch sight of an elegant trogon. The trail parallels the creek, crossing and recrossing, for 4 miles before beginning to climb. (520) 388-8436, www.fs.usda.gov/coronado.

ECHO CANYON LOOP

Perhaps the most popular trail in Chiricahua National Monument, Echo Canyon follows a rocky ridge past the Grottoes, looking like gnawed mini-caves, and squeezes through Wall Street, before dropping into the shady woodland of Echo Park, cooled by a stuttering, spotty little stream. Take the

3.3-mile loop counterclockwise so you'll have an easier return via the Hailstone and Ed Riggs Trails. (520) 824-3560, www.nps.gov/chir.

Where to Eat and Stay

MI CASA RESTAURANT, BENSON

This little mom-and-pop joint in Benson is the very definition of hidden gem. The restaurant only seats twenty-four and is generally packed with locals. The menu features family recipes handed down for generations. Vibrant flavors are artfully presented. The focus is on southern Baja cuisine, but there are Sonoran favorites as well. The chimichangas are plump and delicious, and you can have them Christmas-style, topped by a combination of red and green sauce. 723 W. Fourth St., (520) 245-0343.

LARIAN MOTEL, TOMBSTONE

If Tombstone is known as the "Town Too Tough to Die," the Larian should be called the "Motel Too Good to Pass Up." The classic motor court was built around 1956. Accommodations are always immaculate and just retro enough to give you that warm road-trip feeling. Plush beds, free Wi-Fi, and mini-fridges are just a few creature comforts. Best of all, the Larian borders Tombstone's historic district so everything is just steps from your door. 410 E. Fremont St., (520) 457-2272, www.tombstonemotels.com.

COPPER CITY INN, BISBEE

The inn offers three sumptuous rooms of varying décor, each with a balcony overlooking Main Street. Attention to detail is impeccable, from extra reading lights to slippers in the closet to a library of DVDs to a complimentary bottle of wine. Spacious bathrooms are stocked better than your own at home. Guests are provided with organic coffee and a voucher for a continental breakfast at a gourmet market. 99 Main. St., (520) 432-1418, www.coppercityinn.com.

When You Go

Benson Visitor Center: 249 E. Fourth St., (520) 586-4293, www.bensonvisitorcenter.com.

Old Benson Ice Cream Stop: 102 W. Fourth St., (520) 586-2050.

Horseshoe Café: 154 E. Fourth St., (520) 586-2872.

Tombstone Chamber of Commerce: 109 S. Fourth St., (520) 457-9317, www.tombstonechamber.com.

Boothill Graveyard: Fee. 408 AZ 80, (520) 457-3300, www.tombstoneboothillgiftshop.com.

Tombstone Courthouse State Historic Park: Fee. 223 Toughnut St., (520) 457-3311, www.azstateparks.com.

Bird Cage Theatre: Fee. 535 E. Allen St., (520) 457-3421, www.tombstonebirdcage.com.

O.K. Corral: Fee. 326 E. Allen St., (520) 457-3456, www.okcorral.com.

Bisbee Visitor Center: 478 Dart Rd., (520) 432-3554, www.discoverbisbee.com.

Old Bisbee Ghost Tour: Fee. (520) 432-3308, www.oldbisbeeghosttour.com.

Queen Mine Tour: Fee. 478 Dart Rd., (520) 432-2071, www.queenminetour.com.

Gadsden Hotel: 1046 G Ave., (520) 364-4481, www.thegadsdenhotel.com.

Chiricahua Desert Museum: (575) 557-5757, www.chiricahuadesertmuseum.com.

Portal Peak Lodge: (520) 558-2223, www.portallodge.com.

Chiricahua National Monument: (520) 824-3560, www.nps.gov/chir.

Acknowledgments

The author wishes to thank several people, including Steve Elliott of the Arizona Department of Transportation (ADOT), who took time to answer my many questions. Thanks to the kind folks at University of New Mexico Press for the opportunities. A very big thanks to Mike Koopsen for his enthusiasm for the project and willingness to share his photos, and to Rick Mortensen for his keen photographic eye. The work of Kenneth Lapides is very much appreciated. Gracias to Eric Dickey for the amazing road-trip memories that still shine so brightly all these years later. I'm grateful to Bill Whyte for his friendship and unwavering support. Thanks always to Jill Cassidy, who helped me to discover even more of this remarkable state and was kind enough to keep me employed and out of trouble.

And finally, I am forever indebted to my 2001 Chevy S-10 pickup truck. We spent nearly two decades and more than 250,000 miles rambling around Arizona together and sharing countless adventures. Then afterward, it always brought me home safe and sound. If that's not the definition of a true friend, I don't know what is.

About the Author

Roger Naylor is an award-winning Arizona travel writer. He specializes in state and national parks, lonely hiking trails, twisting back roads, diners with burgers sizzling on the grill, small towns, ghost towns, and pie. In 2018, he was inducted into the Arizona Tourism Hall of Fame. His work has appeared in *Arizona Republic*, *USA Today*, *Go Escape*, *The Guardian*, *Arizona Highways*, *Western Art & Architecture*, and *Route 66 Magazine*. He is a senior writer for the *Bob and Tom Show*, a nationally syndicated radio program. He is the author of *Arizona State Parks: A Guide to Amazing Places in the Grand Canyon State*, *The Amazing Kolb Brothers of Grand Canyon*, *Boots and Burgers: An Arizona Handbook for Hungry Hikers*, *Death Valley: Hottest Place on Earth*, and *Arizona Kicks on Route 66*. For more information, visit RogerNaylor.com.

Roger Naylor has been driving, hiking, and exploring across Arizona since he was a teenager. He considers it a life extremely well spent. Courtesy of Mike Koopsen, Sedona.

SOUTHWEST ADVENTURE SERIES
Ashley M. Biggers, Series Editor

The Southwest Adventure Series provides practical how-to guidebooks for readers seeking authentic outdoor and cultural excursions that highlight the unique landscapes of the American Southwest. Books in the series feature the best ecotourism adventures, world-class outdoor recreation sites, back-road points of interest, and culturally significant archaeological sites, as well as lead readers to the best sustainable accommodations and farm-to-table restaurants in Arizona, Colorado, Nevada, New Mexico, Utah, and Southern California.

Also available in the Southwest Adventure Series:

Arizona State Parks: A Guide to Amazing Places in the Grand Canyon State by Roger Naylor

Eco-Travel New Mexico: 86 Natural Destinations, Green Hotels, and Sustainable Adventures by Ashley M. Biggers

Skiing New Mexico: A Guide to Snow Sports in the Land of Enchantment by Daniel Gibson